KETOGENIC INSTANT POT COOKBOOK

Ketogenic
Instant Pot
Cookbook

Ultra Low Carb Electric Pressure Cooker
Recipes for the Ketogenic Diet

Donna Hunter

Want MORE healthy recipes for FREE?

Double down on healthy living with a full week of fresh, healthy salad recipes. A new salad for every day of the week!

Grab this bonus recipe ebook *free* as our gift to you:

http://salad7.hotbooks.org

Contents

Why Every Keto Dieter Needs an Instant Pot

I'm a woman who has always struggled with my weight, but more than that, I know that the food I've eaten in the past has negatively affected my health. Too much fast food had wreaked havoc on my skin and my energy levels. I wanted to exercise more, but I just never had enough energy to meet my goals. Money had been a big reason for making unhealthy food choices, too, because consistently buying the healthiest food like grass-fed meats and high-quality cooking essentials (like broth) gets expensive after a while.

When I heard about the ketogenic diet, I was intrigued, because most of the diets I've been on have involved tedious calorie-counting and stretches where I feel hungry and tired most of the time. The keto diet is different, because it's about always eating enough healthy fats, a good amount of protein, and very few carbs.

The keto diet taught me that sugar is the enemy, not fat. It's something that makes sense, and after learning how to read labels, I realized just how much sugar is in *everything* we eat. I didn't know how bad my sugar addiction was until I cut out all the processed carbs, refined sugars, and fruit. The first week or so was hard, I admit, but I followed the recommendations on how to get through the "keto flu" by drinking bone broth, eating a few clean carbs like sweet potatoes, and staying hydrated. Water with lemon or cucumber slices was a real life-saver.

Once I started really getting into the keto diet, I saw a lot of blogs about the Instant Pot and pressure-cooking. I did some more research, and found out that pressure-cooking is actually the healthiest cooking method out there, as well as the fastest. Meal planning and prep had been a real pain, especially since my husband isn't totally sold on the keto diet thing yet. I was having to do most of the cooking, and since we both work, there were days when dinner was just canned tuna on some lettuce. As soon as I made my first meal in the IP, I was hooked.

It was just so convenient! I made garlic-lemon chicken thighs, and a sauce that involved just whisking some coconut flour into the cooking liquid after the chicken was cooked. We had a spinach salad on the side, and it was awesome! I've used the poultry and meat/chili settings the most, as well as the steam button if I want to just whip up a big batch of vegetables really quick. I got the 6-quart model, even though it's just me and my husband, because I wanted to be able to make enough for leftovers. I really only have to cook a few times a week now.

The IP also let me make some totally keto-friendly pantry staples like tomato sauce, bone broth, and ketchup. At the store, the keto-friendly brands are usually pretty pricey, but when I make my own, I save a lot. I also save money because I'm not ordering takeout anymore, which even though it seems cheap at the time, it usually costs more per meal than cooking something similar at home. Those savings have allowed me to spend more on foods where quality really matters, like meat. I often buy in bulk and keep it all in the freezer.

How has my life changed since I got the Instant Pot for my keto diet? I've lost weight, but I'm not focused on the numbers on the scale as much anymore, because I just feel so much better. I'm rarely bloated and sluggish, which would happen when I ate a lot of refined and processed carbs like bread and pasta. I don't have cravings for stuff like bread or sugary desserts anymore. I have more energy, and have been exercising more frequently and more efficiently than I ever have before. On weekends, my husband and I will go on long hikes with our dog, and I'm actually excited for our treks. I'm excited about cooking, too, and don't dread the process of grocery shopping or prepping. My husband is able to help more, too, because the Instant Pot is so easy to use, and making good meals has boosted his confidence.

Family and friends have noticed the change, and some are even thinking about switching to a keto diet and getting an Instant Pot, too. I get a lot of compliments from my best friends on how healthy my skin looks, and questions about what's the "secret" to my weight loss. I always tell them - you gotta give up the sugar and carbs. Fat (the healthy ones) are your friend.

What's my favorite thing about the Instant Pot? I'd have to say the consistency. I know that when I put a certain amount of liquid in there, and a few ingredients, everything will always come out the same way pretty much every time. I don't have to babysit a burner or peer into the stove every 5 minutes. It's as if the Instant Pot was designed with the keto diet and my busy lifestyle in mind!

If you are not already a full-fledged keto convert and Instant Pot lover like me, then I believe this is the cookbook that will change that. Whether you're cooking up some simple Riced Cauliflower (pg 40), some decadent (but still healthy!) Bacon-Wrapped Stuffed Chicken Breasts (pg 55), or some spectacular Parmesan Marinara Spaghetti Squash (pg 41), you will be amazed at just how good healthy living can be with this collection of ketogenic recipes and your Instant Pot!

Yours in good health...

Donna Hunter

The Ketogenic Diet: Eating Fat to Get Thin

If you like to search for recipes online, you've probably seen some of them with the label "keto." What does this little four-letter word mean? It's the shortened version of "ketogenic," which refers to the process of "ketosis." This is when the body relies on fat that's been transformed into organic compounds called ketones for fuel. While most people rely on carbs for fuel, ketones are actually a more effective energy source.

How do you get the body to produce ketones and use them for energy? You go on the keto diet. This section explores how people discovered that a low-carb, high-fat diet can treat epilepsy, and that other people can benefit from the results, as well. These benefits include more energy, sharper mental clarity, and weight loss. There are variations of the diet, as well, for those who exercise a lot or athletes, who will need more carbs.

You'll find a full list of "do eat" and "do not eat." The keto diet eliminates all processed food, sugar, and wheat, while it embraces grass-fed meats, full-fat dairy, and dark leafy greens. Some fruit, nuts, and seeds are allowed, but you should always be aware of the carb content. The keto diet has a specific fat, protein, and carb ratio, so your body can stay in ketosis.

Stocking a kitchen can be tricky if you aren't used to eating low-carb, so you'll find helpful tips in this section on how to shop. You'll also learn how to measure your ketone levels, so you can track your progress and make adjustments to your diet as needed. The transition period can be a bit rough, since the body reacts to the initial switch by coming down with flu-like symptoms, but by taking action like staying hydrated and eating enough, you can fight back and put those side effects behind you.

Ready to learn all about the keto diet and how it can change your life? *Let's get started!*

HOW DID THE KETO DIET START?

The ketogenic diet actually began as a fasting regimen. In ancient Greece, Hippocrates - the father of doctors - had a patient who suffered from what we now know as epilepsy. After five straight days of seizures, Hippocrates instructed the man to not eat or drink anything. The seizures stopped, and fasting became common for people with the ailment. Other doctors in ancient India and Persia recorded similar successes, and fasting became the go-to treatment for epilepsy.

Obviously, not eating or drinking anything isn't ideal for most people, so medications were created to treat the symptoms. However, the medications had bad side effects, so in 1911, French doctors created an alternative. They found that a low-calorie diet with lots of vegetables worked somewhat well at suppressing seizures, but it wasn't until 1921 that doctors tweaked the specific balance of the diet. It wasn't enough that the diet was "low-calorie." They changed it to require high amounts of healthy fat, a moderate amount of protein, and very few carbs.

WHY DOES IT WORK?

The reason fasting was used so long and was effective is because fasting forces the body to produce ketones, which change a person's metabolism, which might have an anticonvulsant effect. A high-fat, low-carb diet also encourages the production of ketones, so it mimics the results of fasting, but without the whole starvation side effect.

What are ketones?

When you eat fat, your body needs to break them down before they can be absorbed by cells. Through the process of ketosis, your liver takes fatty acids and turns them into ketones, which are simply organic chemical compounds. Your body actually makes three kinds of ketones during ketosis, with two used for energy. The ketones cycle through the bloodstream and get picked up by cells that need fuel.

THE KETO DIET BREAKDOWN

To get the body to produce ketones, you need to eat a certain ratio of fat, protein, and carbs. The keto diet doesn't require that you count calories, however; it's all about percentages. To reach ketosis, you need 60-75% of your daily calories to come from fat, 15-30% from protein, and just 5-10% from carbs.

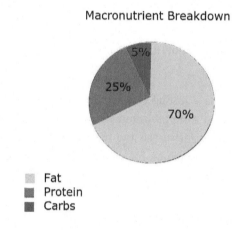

Macronutrient Breakdown

If you're hoping to lose weight, you want 70% of your calories from fat, with 25% from protein, and a meager 5% from carbs. For weight loss, you should also keep an eye on your total calorie count, but you don't need to be counting every one.

To calculate what your macros should be for your specific goals, you can go to a keto calculator online. Set your carb limit at 20 grams, choose the activity level that best represents your lifestyle, and then set your protein level at .8 grams per pound, along with how many pounds you weigh. Calculators will also ask what your health goal is, like weight loss or muscle gain. Once the calculator does its thing, it will let you know your macros for protein and fat.

VARIATIONS ON THE KETO DIET

There are four main versions of the ketogenic diet: the standard ketogenic diet, the targeted ketogenic diet, the cyclical ketogenic diet, and MCT diet. Which one is best for you depends on how much exercise you get.

SKD: This is the normal version of the keto diet. There's nothing special involved, it's just low carbs, high fat, and moderate protein. Most people aim for no more than 20 grams of carbs per day.

TKD: The targeted ketogenic diet requires you eat your carbs before you exercise, so your muscles have enough fuel to work hard. 25-50 grams of carbs a half hour before an intense workout is recommended. If you exercise frequently, this is a good keto diet.

CKD: If you're really active, like an athlete, you should probably be on the cyclical keto diet. You don't stick to the low-carb, high-fat rule every day on this diet variation. Instead, you spend 5-6 days on the keto diet, and then significantly increase your carb intake for 1-2 days.

MCT: If you want to speed up ketosis and have an easier time staying in it, lots of keto experts suggest the MCT diet. The name comes from "medium chain triglycerides," which are oils that include grass-fed butter, coconut oil, and highly-concentrated MCT oils you can buy. Your fat intake is *much* higher on the MCT diet - 87% of your daily calories - with carbs at 5%.

HOW IS THE KETO DIET DIFFERENT THAN GOING PALEO?

The keto diet is often spoken in the same breath with "going Paleo." They do overlap in a lot of ways. Many people like to combine the two diets to get more health benefits, but the diets are not the same. You can be on the keto diet without being Paleo, and vice versa. Here are their main differences:

The keto diet focuses on macronutrients, while being Paleo is about food choices
The keto diet balances protein, fat, and carbs into specific ratios, while the Paleo diet doesn't. The percentages don't matter when you go Paleo. Being on that diet is all about the quality of

food and what was and wasn't available to Paleolithic-era humans. You can adapt the Paleo diet into a low-carb diet to get into ketosis, but that isn't really "Paleo."

The keto diet doesn't cut out ingredients based on when they appeared in the human meal plan
Speaking of Paleolithic-era foods, the keto diet doesn't limit your options based on when humans began eating them. While the Paleo diet doesn't allow sweeteners like stevia or erythritol, both of which are natural, the keto diet embraces them. The only eliminating factor that comes into play with the keto diet is the carb content, not history, of an ingredient.

The keto diet includes (and encourages) dairy
Perhaps the biggest difference between the keto and Paleo diet is that the keto diet *does not* eliminate dairy. Full-fat dairy plays an important role in ketosis, and recipes will include ingredients like full-fat sour cream, yogurt, and more. The Paleo diet eliminates it completely, which is one of the reasons nutritional experts are skeptical about the diet's health benefits.

> ### KETO CELEBRITIES
> The keto diet and variations of it have become one of the most popular diets for celebrities. The media is always wanting to know how the rich and famous keep looking good and keep up with their busy schedules, so food and diet is frequently brought up. Throughout this book you'll learn which celebrities have found success with the high-fat, low-carb mantra of the ketogenic diet.

BENEFITS OF A KETOGENIC DIET
The keto diet has proven to be very effective for people with epilepsy, but what advantages could others without that ailment enjoy if they make the switch to low-carb and high-fat? Here are the most frequently-reported benefits:

Helps with easier weight loss
When you go on a keto diet, you cut out all refined sugar and a lot of the sugar found in fruit, as well. Studies have consistently shown that it's sugar - not fat - that leads to weight gain. Going on the keto diet eliminates the problem, and helps reduce sugar cravings that lead to overeating. The longer you go without refined sugar, the less cravings you have. This makes it much easier to lose weight, and maintain that weight loss, as long as you don't go back to eating sugar.

More energy and sharper mental clarity

Foods with processed, refined carbs and sugar have the tendency to make a person feel heavy and lazy. When you cut out those carbs and rely on lots of fat to feel full, your energy levels go up. The carbs you do eat are slow-burning, which means you have more energy over a longer period of time, without that "crash."

As for mental clarity, the keto diet has proved effective in children with epilepsy, while medications often dull their thinking. The keto diet, on the other hand, is full of brain-boosting foods like avocados and extra virgin olive oil. It makes sense that those foods would help anyone on the diet, and not just those with epilepsy.

> ### KETO CELEBRITIES: LEBRON JAMES
>
> In 2014, LeBron James drastically changed his diet. For 67 straight days, he was on a modified version of the Paleo diet, so it had a ketogenic focus. He didn't eat any carbs, sugar, or dairy. He credited his success that NBA year with his new diet, and lost about 20 pounds. Ketosis can also help athletes with their mental clarity and focus. Athletes on the keto diet have also shown a major difference with those that rely on carbs - their second half of the game is much better. While athletes who rely on carbs and sugar burn everything off and start getting tired, the keto athletes like LeBron stay stable.
>
> #### What does LeBron eat?
>
> Olive oil and lemon vinaigrette dressings on salad, lobster, arugula, squash, zucchini, chicken, grass-fed beef

Less chronic inflammation

For those who have joint pain, inflammation is a familiar word. Inflammation has other symptoms, and if left untreated, it can even cause damage to your organs. Sugar is one of the most inflammatory ingredients out there, so when you're on the keto diet, you eliminate one of the primary triggers of chronic inflammation. Studies have reflected this. The keto diet has also been shown to encourage the body to produce adenosine, which is a pain-relieving chemical that eases joint point.

Helps prevent serious illness

While the science isn't settled on how exactly the keto diet can prevent disease, there's evidence to support that theory. When you eat too many carbs, your body stores too much fat. This can lead to all kinds of diseases, because your brain and other organs are working overtime and very often, literally decaying. The keto diet can help the body burn off that stored fat. Studies have also shown that burning ketones for energy instead of glucose has a healing effect on the brain, which the MCT keto diet might even help treat Alzheimer's.

IS THE KETO DIET GOOD FOR ATHLETES?

One of the big questions about the keto diet is if it's good for athletes. Typically, athletes eat a lot of carbs because they burn up quickly and fuel their bodies. Carbs are also important in recovery, so people are worried that a keto diet will lead to muscle damage. What do the studies say?

One study had ultra-endurance athletes eat low-carb for 20 months, and then run for three hours against athletes eating a high-carb diet. The keto athletes burned 2-3 times more fat. Most importantly, they used and gained the same amount of muscle glycogen, which is the name for the body's stored carbs. This means the keto athletes weren't at risk for damaging their muscles. Other studies have shown promise, too, so you don't have to sacrifice performance if you're active and wanting to try the keto diet.

Keep in mind, however, that there are certain exercises that are better than others when you're on the keto diet:

Aerobic exercises- These types of exercises are slow and cardio-based. They're also good for burning fat, so they're a good fit for keto athletes.

Stability exercises - Both low-carb and high-carb diets provide enough energy for these core-based balance workouts.

Flexibility exercises - Any joint pain will make these exercises hard, and since the keto diet is really good at reducing the inflammation that causes the pain, you'll be able to do more of these on the keto diet.

Anaerobic exercises - Carbs fuel these types of workouts, which include interval training and fast, intense bursts of energy. The keto diet isn't a good fit for these types of exercises, so if you want to engage in these types of workouts, the TKD or CKD keto diet is best.

CRITICISMS OF THE KETO DIET

All diets have problems that nutritional experts like to point out. It's important to know what they have to say because the keto diet might not be the best choice for you. Here are the most common issues that the keto diet has:

It's very restrictive

There are a lot of ingredients and foods you have to eliminate on the keto diet. A lot of them are the most convenient options, like anything that comes in a package. You are eliminating an entire food group - grain - which takes up a big chunk of most people's diets. A restrictive diet is hard to maintain, so it's a flaw that should be acknowledged.

Switching to keto is hard

Adopting a keto diet is hard for most people, because we rely so much on carbs. Cutting them out of your diet can trigger a "keto flu," which we will talk about more in depth later. Changing your meal plans, restocking your kitchen, and having to change how you eat outside of your home are all challenges that often discourage people from sticking to the keto diet.

It can cause micronutrient deficiency

Nutritionists are always wary of diets that cut out whole food groups, and the fact that the keto diet eliminates grains concerns them. You could be at risk for micronutrient deficiency, which is when you aren't getting enough of a specific vitamin or mineral. Supplements can help with this imbalance, but since it's always better to get nutrients from food sources, many experts don't like the ketogenic diet.

It can cause ketoacidosis

Your body can get too much of a good thing. When you have too many ketones, your blood becomes acidic, which is a major problem for people with diabetics. It can actually kill you. Symptoms of ketoacidosis include stomach pain, vomiting, and dehydration. This makes the keto diet risky for diabetics, so monitoring your ketone levels is essential. We'll discuss how to do this later.

FOOD YOU CAN EAT

So, you know what the keto diet is, the benefits, and the downsides. What can you actually eat on the diet? What kinds of meals will you be cooking for you and your family? Even though the keto diet is considered "restrictive," there's actually a lot of variety in terms of ingredients and meal possibilities. Here's a comprehensive list of what's allowed:

Proteins

The key to proteins is to get the highest-quality you can afford. That means wild-caught, pasture-raised, and grass-fed. You don't want any nasty artificial ingredients or additives. Another tip to keep in mind is to watch your consumption of red meat. Some people go a bit overboard, and forget about fish. Try to eat fish at least 3 times a week when you're on the keto diet.

Poultry - *Free-range chicken, duck, turkey, bone broth, etc.*

Eggs - *Free-range and organic*

Beef - *Grass-fed steak, roasts, stew, and ground, beef bone broth*

Pork - *Ground, pork loin, pork chops, ham, tenderloin, bacon, etc.*

Fish - *Wild-caught and sustainable salmon, halibut, cod, mahi-mahi, tuna, trout, etc.*

Shellfish - *Clams, crab, scallops, lobster, etc.*

Organ meat - *Heart, kidney, tongue, liver, etc.*

Other meats- *Lamb, veal, goat*

Nut butters - *Unsweetened, all-natural peanut, almond and macadamia nut butter*

KETO CELEBRITIES: HALLE BERRY

Known for her eternal youthfulness as well as her acting skill, Halle Berry went on the ketogenic diet to have better control of her type 1 diabetes, which she's had since she was 19 years old. Staying in good shape is very important for someone with that disease, and with two kids, Halle intends to be around for a long time. She talked about her diet on Live! with Kelly and Ryan, saying she eats "healthy fats all day long," and doesn't eat any sugar. She's also very active, and has a personal trainer who helps her with cardio and bodyweight exercises.

What does Halle eat?

Coconut oil, butter, avocado, grilled tuna, vegetable protein, sugar substitute xylitol

---

Fats and oils

Both saturated and monounsaturated fats are allowed on the keto diet. No trans-fat, however.

Avocado oil - *monounsaturated*

Almond oil - *monounsaturated*

Avocado - *monounsaturated*

Coconut oil - *saturated*

Coconut butter - *saturated*

Cocoa butter - *saturated*

Duck fat - *saturated*

Ghee - *saturated*

Grass-fed butter - *saturated*

Olive oil - *monounsaturated/cold-pressed is best*

KETO CELEBRITIES: KOURTNEY KARDASHIAN

Kourtney's diets and famous "detoxes" are very strict. She has regular 16-19 hour fasts where all she'll consume is water and bone broth. She also only eats three meals a day without snacking, which is not something that's required on the keto diet. Being in constant ketosis is a good way to detox bad stuff like metals from the body, which is what motivated Kourtney. She consulted her doctor first, and recommends that everyone do this before trying something extreme.

What does Kourtney eat?

Chicken, fish, salmon, cauliflower and broccoli rice, spaghetti squash, roasted asparagus, avocado smoothies with MCT oil and bone broth powder

---

Dairy

High-quality, full-fat dairy is an important part of the ketogenic diet, but cow's milk has too much sugar. Instead you'll be drinking nut milk that does not include carrageenan. For cheeses, go with blocks as often as you can since pre-shredded cheese uses potato starch to prevent clumping.

Coconut cream

Cottage cheese

Cream cheese

Greek yogurt

Heavy whipping cream

Mascarpone cheese

Mozzarella cheese

Parmesan cheese

Ricotta cheese

Swiss cheese

Unsweetened almond, coconut, or macadamia nut milk

Vegetables

Organic vegetables are the best. Both fresh and frozen is acceptable, since they have the same nutritional value. You want dark, leafy greens as much as possible, which higher-carb vegetables like potatoes and squash should be avoided.

Cabbage	Onion - best in moderation
Cauliflower	Radishes
Cucumber	Sea vegetables - nori + kombu
Celery	Swiss chard
Bell peppers - best in moderation	Spinach
Broccoli	Lettuce
Garlic	Tomatoes - best in moderation
Kale	Zucchini

Fruit

Most fruit is too high in sugar for the keto diet, so the list of fruit you can eat is fairly short. Fruit juice is also way too high in sugar, though it can be used as a sweetener in moderation.

Avocado	Cherries - best if rarely eaten
Berries - raspberries, blackberries, blueberries, strawberries, cranberries	Peaches -best if rarely eaten
	Watermelon - best if rarely eaten
Citrus fruit - lemon, lime, orange	

Nuts + seeds

The only nut that's totally forbidden on the keto diet are legumes, because they're too high in carbs. In general, nuts should always be eaten in moderation. The best nut for the ketogenic diet is probably the macadamia nut, because of its high fat content.

Almonds - best in moderation	Macadamia nuts - good keto nut
Brazil nuts - good keto nut	Pecans - good keto nut
Chia seeds	Pumpkin seeds
Flax seeds	Sunflower seeds -best in moderation

Baking supplies

Traditional baking supplies like flour and sugar are not allowed on the keto diet, so you will be relying on alternative flours and natural, zero-calorie sweeteners.

Almond flour

Aluminum-free baking powder and soda

Blends - Sukrin Gold, Truvia, In The Raw, etc.

Coconut flour - absorbs more liquid than other flours

Dark + natural cocoa powder

Erythritol - goes through body undigested + doesn't absorb carbs

Monk fruit - 300x sweeter than sugar

Psyllium husk - 100% fiber used as thickener

Stevia - comes in liquid and granule form

KETO CELEBRITIES: TIM TEBOW

Former football player and current baseball player Tim Tebow is a big believer in the keto diet. One look at him and it's clear that the fear that a keto diet breaks down muscle is not founded on facts. In an interview with GQ, Tim raved about the keto diet, saying that avocados are his favorite part of it. He eats around four a day. He also emphasized eating whenever he was hungry to keep his metabolism going, and pointed out that people make bad food decisions when they're hungry.

What does Tim eat?

Avocado-spinach-ginger smoothies, stevia, unsweetened almond milk, bulletproof coffee (coffee with butter), eggs

---

Drinks

Most commercial beverages are not good for a keto diet, but there are some you can have. Water is always best, and unsweetened, herbal teas are also encouraged. You can have alcohol, but very rarely.

Hard liquors - in extreme moderation

Light beer - in extreme moderation

Sparkling water + seltzers

Tea - unsweetened + herbal

Unsweetened coconut water

Unsweetened coffee

Water

Wine - in extreme moderation

Keto-friendly brands

Here is a beginner's list of keto-friendly brands. Always read the labels to get familiar with keto-compliant ingredients, and to keep track of the amount of carbs, protein, and fat in each item.

StarKist tuna packets

Trader Joe's brand crab cakes

Trader Joe's brand chicken and turkey burgers

Trader Joe's brand mahi-mahi and salmon burgers

Healthy Choice grilled chicken & broccoli alfredo (4 grams of net carbs)

Healthy Choice grilled chicken pesto & vegetables (6 grams of net carbs)

Gordon's all-natural grilled fish fillets (1 net carb per serving)

Kerrygold grass-fed butter

Organic Valley grass-fed butter

Darigold heavy cream

Silk unsweetened almond milk

Trader Joe's brand almond milk

Native Forest coconut milk and cream

So Delicious coconut products

Coconut Secret raw coconut cream

Organic Valley cottage cheese

Siggi's whole milk yogurt (comes in vanilla, strawberry, plain, rhubarb, and mixed berry)

Justin's nut butters

Emerald 100-calorie nut packs

Quest Bars (less than 3 net carbs per serving)

Moon Cheese snacks

Babybel cheeses

Annie Chun's seaweed snacks

Bob's Red Mill (almond flour, flax meal, etc.)

Now Foods (psyllium powder, flaxseeds, erythritol)

Smucker's sugar-free fruit preserves (with Truvia)

Nielsen-Massey flavor extracts (maple, almond, lemon, cherry, etc.)

Sukrin Gold (brown sugar substitute)

SweetLeaf (stevia)

Walden Farms sugar-free ketchup

Annie's Naturals organic horseradish mustard (no sugar)

Eden's yellow mustard

Red Boat fish sauce

Bragg's apple cider vinegar

Coconut Secret coconut aminos

Frank's hot sauce (no sugar)

WHAT YOU *CAN'T* EAT

The reason for eliminating foods on the keto diet is because they make it difficult to get into ketosis and stay there because of their carb and sugar content. These forbidden foods also probably have too many artificial ingredients and are linked to health problems.

All processed meats - hot dogs, packaged sausages, grain-fed meats, etc.

All grains - wheat, corn, quinoa, buckwheat, oats, barley, rice, etc.

Anything processed + packaged - fast food, baked goods, ice cream, wheat gluten, MSG, "diet" food

Inflammatory oils - soybean, corn, canola, grapeseed, sesame, peanut, sunflower oil

Milk + dairy marked "low fat" - butter substitutes, fat-free yogurts, low-fat cream cheese, regular milk, skim milk, margarine, etc.

Beans + legumes - kidney beans, black beans, lentils, fava beans, white beans, chickpeas, peas, etc.

Starchy veggies - corn, sweet potatoes, butternut squash, acorn squash, artichokes, potatoes, yams

Most fruits - bananas, apples, grapes, mangos, smoothies, fruit syrups, dried fruit

Refined sweeteners - white sugar, raw sugar, cane sugar, maple syrup, agave, corn syrup

Artificial sweeteners - splenda, equal, saccharin, sucralose, anything with aspartame

Bottled condiments - ketchup, mustard, salad dressings

Most alcohol - beer, cocktails, flavored liqueurs, wine coolers, flavored beers, etc.

HOW TO STOCK A KETOGENIC KITCHEN + PANTRY

When switching to a keto diet, most people find it's better to go 100% keto right away. If you transition more slowly, you'll have to wait longer for the benefits, and it will be harder to stay disciplined and kick cravings to the curb. Going all-keto right away means you'll need to restock your kitchen, from your pantry to your fridge.

Get rid of all non-keto food

The first thing to do is clear out all the non-keto food. If ingredients are unopened, donate them to a food shelf. If they are opened, see if you have friends or family who can use them. You want to get rid of all temptations right away, and not accidentally use something that will kick you out of ketosis.

Make a list of keto kitchen staples

The next step is to replenish your must-haves with the keto alternatives. This includes baking supplies, oils, frozen food, and canned food. Depending on what you like and use a lot, your list might be slightly different. You should also have a variety of herbs and spices, which you probably didn't have to get rid of, because they're already keto-friendly.

Here's a sample of what should be in your home at all times:

Proteins

Organic chicken (breasts, thighs, etc.)

Ground grass-fed beef

Ground turkey

Frozen fish fillets

High-quality canned tuna

Nitrate-free, high-quality bacon

Fats + Oils

Coconut oil

Olive oil (cold-pressed)

Dairy

Heavy cream

Grass-fed butter

Plain, whole-milk Greek yogurt

A soft cheese (full-fat mozzarella, ricotta, etc.)

A hard cheese (in block form)

Non-dairy

Full-fat coconut milk

Unsweetened almond milk

Organic coconut cream

Fruit

Avocados

No-sugar fruit preserves/marmalade

Raspberries, Strawberries, and Blueberries (fresh or frozen)

Vegetables

Cauliflower

Celery

Cucumbers

Dark leafy greens (Swiss chard, kale, and/or spinach)

Onions

Garlic

Zucchini

Nuts + seeds

Whole almonds

Unsweetened almond nut butter

Pecans

Macadamia nuts or Brazil nuts

Baking/cooking supplies

Almond flour

Aluminum-free baking powder

Beef/chicken bone broth

Coconut flour

High-quality canned tomatoes

Dark baking chocolate

Flaxmeal

Homemade ketchup and yellow mustard

Psyllium husk

Rodelle pure vanilla extract (sugar-free)

Sukrin Gold (brown sugar substitute)

Stevia + erythritol (or a blend of both)

Unsweetened dark cocoa powder

Unsweetened shredded coconut

Go shopping

Before you go shopping, you want to make a list of all the staples and ingredients for the meals you want to make that week. There will probably be some overlap, but not necessarily, which is why you want to make two lists to be sure not to miss anything. Think about what you can buy in bulk, if you use it a lot, and what's in season. If you aren't sure if the store has an item, you can call ahead and ask. That will save you a lot of time roaming around the aisles.

Learn how to save money

Since keto-friendly foods can be expensive, you should also familiarize yourself with coupons, where to get the best ones, and online shopping. A lot of people on the keto diet order grass-fed meat in bulk, because it ends up being cheaper per pound than at the store. You can also check out local farmer's markets, if you have them, for fresh produce.

Learn how to read labels

The final tip on buying keto groceries is to learn how to read labels. When you take a closer look at a label, you will see "total carbs" or "net carbs." If the brand was made in the USA, it usually says "total carbs," while brands from the UK will say "net carbs." Total carbs represents starch carbs + sugar carbs + fiber, while "net carbs" subtracts the fiber from the total amount. When you're aiming for a daily 20 carbs on your keto diet, that's *net carbs*.

Other words you want to be on the lookout for on labels are all the different words for sugar. You should avoid malt syrup, coconut sugar, corn syrup, monosaccharide, lactose, maltose, and sugar alcohols. Here are some other words for wheat, corn, and soy that you should know:

Wheat + gluten

Dextrin, caramel color, artificial flavoring, malt, hydrolyzed wheat protein, hydrolyzed wheat starch, hydrolyzed plant protein (HPP), hydrolyzed vegetable protein (HVP), maltodextrin, vegetable starch, natural flavoring

Corn

Dextrose, food starch, mazena, modified gum starch, sorbitol, MSG, xanthan gum, xylitol

Soy

Miso, stabilizer, tamari, tempeh, tofu, vegetable broth, textured vegetable protein (TVP), vegetable gum

How to Measure Your Ketones

Once you start the keto diet, you'll probably want to know what your ketone level is. If you are diabetic, it's basically required to monitor your ketones, because if the level is too high, it can put your life in danger. There are three ways to test ketones:

Urine strips

A good ol' fashioned urine strip measures the level of your acetoacetate ketones. This is a good method if you are just beginning ketosis, because once you've been in ketosis for a while, your body doesn't actually excrete a lot of the acetoacetate ketone. This is because your body is using the ketone.

A blood meter

Testing your blood measures levels of the beta-hydroxybutyrate ketone (BHB). This test is more accurate than a urine strip, but more expensive. A lot of people also don't like the idea of pricking your finger, but if you are a diabetic, you're probably used to it.

A breath test

The breath test measures the acetone ketone. While this ketone isn't actually that important in ketosis, its levels do line up pretty closely with your BHB ketone level. These tests are not as cheap as urine strips, but you can keeping using it, so you just have to buy it once.

Interpreting the Results

The units most commonly used to measure ketone levels are mmol/L, which means millimole per liter. The ideal ketone level for you depends on what your goal is.

For weight loss - above 0.5 mmol/L

For better athletic performance - above 0.5 mmol/L

For improved mental capability - 1.5 - 3 mmol/L

Therapeutic/help with mental illness symptoms - 3 -6 mmol/L

For diabetics, if your ketone levels are between 0.6-1.5 mmol/L, talk to your doctor, because you're teetering on the edge of too many ketones. If you reach 1.6 mmol/L and above, you're at risk for ketoacidosis. Anything 3 mmol/L and higher requires *immediate* medical treatment.

Treating the "Keto Flu"

When your body is switching into ketosis, it can trigger unpleasant symptoms. Because your body is working overtime and adjusting to your new diet, you might experience fatigue, headaches, nausea, and other flu-like effects. For most people, this "keto flu" only lasts a week or so. How rough it is depends on how many carbs you're used to getting in your diet. If you find the "flu" symptoms are disrupting the normal flow of your life, here are some tips on how to feel better:

Stay hydrated

When your body transitions into ketosis, you use a lot more water than usual. Staying hydrated is super important, so you want to drink more than you normally would. Always carry a water bottle with you. Another way to stay hydrated *and* replenish electrolytes is to drink chicken broth that you've added a high-quality salt to. Salted chicken broth has helped lots of people with headaches, joint cramping, and fatigue.

Eat as many healthy fats and protein as you need

When you cut out carbs like grain, you are going to need to eat more of healthy fats and protein to feel as full. This is where choosing not to count calories pays off, because you can eat as much as you need for energy. If weight loss is a goal, you'll eventually need to be aware of your calorie intake, but for the first few weeks on the keto diet, just focus on not eating carbs.

Try some light exercise

Exercise actually speeds up ketosis, but you do want to keep it light while you're transitioning, because your energy levels won't be as high. If you try to do intense workouts, you will be discouraged, and in the worst case scenario, you will yourself sick. Instead, think yoga and Pilates. Those types of exercises tend to force the body to rely on fat as fuel, so you are helping along the transition.

Start the morning with MCT oil

Even if you aren't on the MCT keto diet, consuming some high-quality coconut oil in the morning can make the transition go faster. Mix a glass of water and two teaspoons of coconut oil, and drink it with your breakfast. MCT oils are more concentrated, but the manufacturing process is sometimes iffy, so be aware of that.

Consume some carbs

The keto flu can be tough if you have been really reliant on carbs. If you are feeling really ill, eat some carbs. It slows down ketosis, but it's worth it because you'll feel much better. Your carb choices are important, too, so eat foods like grapes, nectarines, sweet potatoes, or parsnips. These are slow-burning, clean carbs that won't derail the ketosis process like bread or other refined carbs will.

What's The Big Deal about the Instant Pot?

As soon as people began cooking with pots, it didn't take long for them to realize that putting a lid on speed up the boiling process. However, it wasn't until 1679 that someone created an airtight seal. Denis Papin wanted to create a device that the poor classes could use to cook cheap cuts of meat down into "bone jelly." That would require extremely hot temperatures higher than water's boiling point. To achieve that, he created a special airtight seal on a giant pot. After cooking a meal for the king using his "bone digester," Papin impressed people, but the pot was too expensive, large, and dangerous for mass distribution.

The idea of the airtight seal emerged again much later during the Napoleonic Wars. When Napoleon issued a request for a way to preserve food for his soldiers, a confectioner invented the pressure canner, which involved submerging sealed glass jars into scalding water. His technique was adopted by the French army, and he opened the first cannery.

The pressure cooker as we know it showed up at the 1939 World's Fair. Till then, there had been no pressure-cooking device meant for everyday meals. The first electric cooker was patented in 1991 in China, following years of just stovetop cookers. The Instant Pot, the most popular electric pressure cooker on Amazon, came out in 2010. What sets this cooker apart from the others is its user-friendly design and the fact it can be used as a pressure cooker, slow cooker, and yogurt maker.

KETO CELEBRITIES: TIM FERRISS

Author of the "The Four-Hour Work Week" and "The Four-Hour Body," Tim is a big promoter of the keto diet as well as his own "slow-carb diet". He's tried a *ton* of other diets, but credits the keto diet with helping to treat his Lyme disease. He combines the traditional low-carb, high-fat diet with fasting. He will go multiple days without food every 4 months. His reasons? Autophagy, which is triggered by ketosis and reaches its peak during fasting, is the body's way of "cleaning out" cells. Ferriss credits Dr. Dominic D'Agostino for his views on the keto diet.

What does Tim eat?

Grass-fed beef, guacamole, eggs, chicken, big salads

How the Instant Pot works

The Instant Pot and all pressure cookers have the same basic operation: an airtight seal on a pot causes pressure to build up, which causes liquid to reach higher temperatures than the normal boiling point. Instead of topping out at 212 °F, pressure cookers let liquid boil to 250°F. This translates into faster cooking.

The exact amount of pressure in a pressure cooker varies. PCs are measured in PSIs, which stands for "pounds per square inch." Stovetop cookers have the highest PSI at about 15, while the Instant Pot has 10-11 PSI. This makes it a little slower than a stovetop cooker, but still much faster than other cooking methods.

How fast? Cooking a recipe in an IP takes ½ or even ⅓ of the time it would in an oven. The exact time depends on where you are above or below sea level. The higher you are above sea level, the longer it takes for water to boil. For 1,000 feet you are above sea level, you should on 5% of the pressure cooker recipe's cooking time. A pressure cooker also needs a certain amount of time to reach pressure, but most recipes don't include that in the recipe, because it varies so much based on what you're cooking and where you are.

What happens to the pressure in a cooker when a recipe's cook time is up? There are two ways to release pressure. The first way is to remove the cooker from the heat, or, in the case of the Instant Pot, turn it off. The pressure will slowly release from the cooker by itself, thanks to specifically-designed holes. The second method is to "quick-release" the pressure. You do this by turning a steam release handle to "venting." Steam comes out quickly, and once the pressure is gone, you can then open the cooker.

The Instant Pot up close

The Instant Pot brands makes several models with different price points and features. The Duo Series 7-in-1 is very popular, because it has a yogurt setting and gives you the ability to choose between low and high pressure. It comes in 5, 6, or 8 quarts. Most families (of four) like the 6-quart, though the 8-quart has the advantage of making enough food for large groups and leftovers. In terms of price, the 7-in-1 in 6 quarts is about $100.

The Ultra 10-in-1 is one of the most impressive electric cookers out there. It has 16 preset programs including one for yogurt, for eggs, for cake, and a sterilize setting. It also gives you more control over temperature settings. The most expensive cooker, the Instant Pot Smart, has Bluetooth capabilities and an app that lets you control the pot from your phone.

What model is best for you depends on your needs and budget. No matter what model you get, you will probably need *at least* a 6-quart. If you only cook for one person, a 5-quart might be enough, but you'll likely not be able to cook food for more than two people at the most. A 6-

quart is common for families of four, though if you like to make enough food for leftovers, go with an 8-quart.

Learning the programs

The programs on the IP are one of its biggest selling points. They are all preset with pressure and time, so by selecting the right one for your recipe, it takes out all the guesswork.

Soup - *high pressure for 30 minutes*

Meat/stew - *high pressure for 35 minutes*

Bean/chili - *high pressure for 30 minutes*

Poultry - *high pressure for 15 minutes*

Rice - *low pressure for time IP calculates, based on amount of water and rice*

Multigrain- *high pressure for 40 minutes*

Porridge - *high pressure for 20 minutes*

Steam -*low pressure for 10 minutes*

Slow cook - *turns the IP into a slow cooker*

Sauté - *preheats the cooker, used to sauté ingredients before pressure-cooking*

Pressure - *choose between high or low pressure*

"-" and "+" buttons - *push to adjust time for manual or timer*

Manual - *adjust time and pressure manually on the cooker*

Adjust - *adjust the "sauté" function, push once for browning and twice for simmering*

Timer - *delay cooking for time you choose using the "-" or "+" buttons*

Yogurt - *turns the cooker into a yogurt maker, used exclusively for yogurt*

Keep warm/cancel - *cooker automatically switches to this program after cook time is up, can also be used to turn off cooker or cancel program*

Taking the IP apart

The IP has a lot of parts, at first glance, but most of them are attached, and they work all by themselves. Here are descriptions of the Instant Pot parts, so you can know what your device is made of:

Base & heating unit - *where the IP generates its heat*

Control panel - *where the programs and time are displayed*

Control box - *the cooker's brain*

Exterior pot - *the outside "shell" of the cooker, holds the inner pot*

Inner pot - *holds food, and is dishwasher-safe*

Lid - *goes on top of the pot*

Steam release handle - turn to "venting" to release pressure manually, or "sealed" to build pressure

Steam release - small hole where pressure escapes when you turn the steam release handle

Float valve - tiny pin that is either popped up to show that pressure is reached, or down to indicate that pressure is gone

Exhaust valve - safety feature that prevents excess pressure build-up

Sealing ring - also known as the gasket, a silicone ring that what gives lid its airtight seal on the pot, can be removed from the lid for cleaning

Seal support - safety feature

Grommet - safety feature

Anti-block shield - safety feature that prevents overheating

KETO CELEBRITIES: THE NAVY SEALS

One of Tim Ferriss's mentors, Dominic D'Agostino, was once asked to solve a problem that the Navy SEALS experienced. The divers use a rebreather for long dives, but they were getting oxygen-toxicity seizures, which are extremely dangerous. When researching how to prevent this from happening, Dr. D'Agostino read about how the ketogenic diet is used to treat epilepsy. He saw how ketones are capable of calming down nerve transmissions in the brain that cause seizures. In 2015, the divers were assigned the keto diet, and their seizures stopped.

What do SEALS eat?

Shakes with whey protein, unsweetened almond milk, heavy cream, summer squash, baked salmon, spinach, butter, olive oil

---

BENEFITS OF USING AN INSTANT POT

There are so many reasons to love the Instant Pot. If you've ever read reviews about this brand, you'll find that most people rave about it. Here's a sample of the kinds of benefits you can enjoy with the IP:

Healthier food

Studies have shown that pressure cooking consistently tops the list of healthiest cooking methods. This is because the fast cooking time means more nutrients are preserved in food, especially vegetables. You can expect ingredients to keep 80-95% of their vitamins and minerals, while food like beans and grains become easier to digest.

Faster food

How fast is fast? Rice and steel-cut oats, foods that usually take a long time, can be finished in 6 minutes. Stews, soups, and chilies that take hours can be done and taste just as rich in 60 or so minutes. This makes cooking at home much more convenient, which is crucial for families that have busy schedules.

Versatile meals

If you get tired of having the same meals over and over again, the Instant Pot is the perfect tool to shake things up. You can cook a wide variety of one-pot meals like chicken and vegetables, pasta, casseroles, soups, and more. You can even cook desserts when you have accessories like steamer baskets and baking dishes that fit in the inner pot. Variety is the spice of life, and the IP lets you embrace that variety without a ton of fancy kitchen equipment.

Convenient, easy cooking

Cooking is intimidating for some people. They're afraid of the oven and stovetop, and prefer to stick the microwave and its panel of buttons. The IP is controlled with a panel of buttons, too, but the meals it produces are much healthier. There isn't a steep learning curve with an electric pressure cooker, which is why it's become more popular than the stovetop version, so even if you've never used one, it's easy to jump on board.

THE KETO DIET AND YOUR INSTANT POT

The Instant Pot is the perfect tool for those on the keto diet. It preserves more nutrients than any other cooking method, which is very important when you're on the keto diet and need to get as much nutrition as possible from veggie and meat. The IP is also easy to use and lets you cook healthy meals faster, so even if you are very busy and haven't had time to cook in the past, pressure-cooking makes it more convenient. As you're about to discover when you enjoy the mouth-watering recipes you'll find in the rest of this cookbook, with the ketogenic diet and your Instant Pot, you really can have it all!

Vegetables

Frittata with Cheese and Broccoli

Serves: 4 / Preparation time: 10 minutes / Cooking time: 30 minutes

This versatile egg dish can be served for any meal. Serve alongside bacon or sausage for breakfast or brunch, or pair with a leafy green salad for lunch or dinner. Many herbs and spices will deliciously complement broccoli. Try using basil, chives, marjoram, thyme or sage in place of the dill.

2 tablespoons butter

1 onion, diced

4 cloves garlic, peeled and minced

2 cups bite-size broccoli florets

8 eggs

½ cup plain whole-milk yogurt

½ teaspoon dried dill

8 ounces mild cheddar cheese, shredded

Salt and freshly ground black pepper, to taste

- Set Instant Pot to sauté, melt butter and cook onion and garlic until transparent, stirring occasionally, about 5 minutes. Add broccoli florets and cook until slightly softened, about 4 minutes. Remove broccoli mixture from pot and set aside.

- Whisk eggs and yogurt until thoroughly combined. Stir in cheese and broccoli mixture and season to taste with salt and pepper.

- Select a casserole dish that fits inside the Instant Pot. Grease casserole dish with butter or spray with nonstick cooking spray. Pour egg mixture into casserole dish and cover with aluminum foil.

- Set trivet inside pot and pour about 1 cup water into pot. Carefully set casserole dish on trivet. Secure pot lid, close pressure valve and cook on manual setting until done, about 20 minutes. When cooking time ends, let pressure release naturally.

- Using oven mitts, carefully remove casserole from instant pot. Cut frittata into wedges and serve immediately, or let cool. Enjoy!

Per Serving: Calories: 462; Total Fat: 34g; Saturated Fat: 16g; Protein: 28g; Carbs: 7g; Fiber: 2g; Sugar: 2g

Cauliflower "Mac" and Cheese

Serves: 4 / Preparation time: 15 minutes / Cooking time: 5 minutes

You won't miss the macaroni in this cheesy dish. Any flavorful cheese that melts easily, such as Gouda, Colby or Fontana, could be used in this recipe. For an extra keto boost, sprinkle with diced ham or crumbled bacon before serving.

1 large head cauliflower (about 3 pounds), cut into bite-size pieces

1 tablespoon butter

½ teaspoon salt

1 3-ounce package cream cheese, cut into pieces

1 cup plain whole-milk yogurt

2 ounces sharp cheddar cheese, shredded

2 ounces white cheddar cheese, shredded

¼ teaspoon garlic powder

Salt and freshly ground black pepper, to taste

- Pour 1 cup water into Instant Pot. Place cauliflower pieces in steamer basket and set in pot. Secure pot lid, close pressure valve and cook on steam setting until softened, about 5 minutes. When cooking time ends, let pressure release naturally.

- Remove steamer basket, drain water from pot and set pot to warm. Mix cauliflower, butter, salt, cream cheese, yogurt, cheddar cheeses and garlic powder in pot, season to taste with salt and pepper and stir until cheese is melted.

- Serve immediately and enjoy!

Per Serving: Calories: 280; Total Fat: 19; Saturated Fat: 15g; Protein: 13g; Carbs: 14g; Fiber: 5g; Sugar: 6g

Riced Cauliflower

Serves: 4 / Preparation time: 5 minutes / Cooking time: 15 minutes

Riced cauliflower is versatile and tasty, standing in for rice for people cutting down on carbohydrate consumption. Serve cauliflower rice right from the pot as a tasty side dish, or use it as a base for creamy curries, spicy sauces and rich stews.

1 large head cauliflower (about 3 pounds), cut into large chunks

1 teaspoon lemon juice

2 tablespoons butter

½ teaspoon salt

- Pour 1 cup of water into Instant Pot. Place cauliflower in steamer basket and set in pot. Drizzle lemon juice over cauliflower.

- Secure pot lid, close pressure valve and cook on manual setting for 1 minute. Carefully turn venting knob from sealing to venting position for a quick pressure release.

- Remove steamer basket, drain water from pot, and set pot to sauté.

- Melt butter in pot, add cauliflower and salt, and mash cauliflower to desired consistency with a fork or a potato masher. Fluff cauliflower with a fork if necessary. Serve and enjoy!

Per Serving: Calories: 103; Total Fat: 6g; Saturated Fat: 4g; Protein: 4g; Carbs: 11g; Fiber: 5g; Sugar: 5g

Parmesan Marinara Spaghetti Squash

Serves: 4 / Preparation time: 15 minutes / Cooking time: 30 minutes

Unlike conventional pasta, spaghetti squash is very low in carbohydrates. Its mild flavor pairs it perfectly with this light and flavorful marinara sauce. Serve a leafy green salad on the side to round out a tasty summer dinner.

1 large spaghetti squash

1 tablespoon olive oil

¼ cup finely chopped onion

¼ cup finely chopped red bell pepper

1 can (28 ounces) crushed tomatoes

1 can (6 ounces) tomato paste

1 teaspoon Italian herb blend

½ cup finely grated Parmesan cheese

1 tablespoon butter

Salt and freshly ground pepper, to taste

- Pierce spaghetti squash skin all over with a fork or the tip of a sharp knife. Place squash in steamer basket and set in Instant Pot. Secure pot lid, close pressure valve and cook on high setting for 20 minutes. When cooking time ends, let pressure release naturally.

- Remove steamer basket and set squash aside. Drain water from pot, set pot to sauté and cook onion and bell pepper in olive oil until translucent, stirring frequently. Add tomatoes, tomato paste, and herb blend to pot, season to taste with salt and pepper and mix thoroughly. Secure pot lid, close pressure valve and cook on high setting for 8 minutes.

- While sauce is cooking, cut squash in half. Scoop out and discard squash seeds. Scrape squash flesh from shell into strings with a fork. Toss squash with butter and season to taste with salt and pepper. At the end of sauce cooking time, let pressure release naturally.

- Divide squash among serving plates, drizzle with sauce and garnish with grated Parmesan cheese. Serve remaining sauce and cheese on the side and enjoy!

Per Serving: Calories: 300; Total Fat: 12g; Saturated Fat: 5g; Protein: 2g; Carbs: 9g; Fiber: 2g; Sugar: 4g

Creamy Kale Soup

Serves: 4 / Preparation time: 5 minutes / Cooking time: 5 minutes

Serve this savory soup as a complement to ham, chicken or any roasted meat. To make the soup a hearty main dish, add 1 pound ground beef or Italian sausage to pot while sautéing the onion and garlic.

1 onion, diced

4 stalks celery, trimmed and chopped

8 cloves garlic, peeled and minced

1 tablespoon butter

1 package (16 ounces) frozen chopped kale

1 package (16 ounces) frozen cauliflower florets

4 cups beef or chicken stock

1 tablespoon balsamic vinegar

Salt and freshly ground pepper, to taste

½ cup heavy cream

4 tablespoons finely grated Parmesan cheese

- In Instant Pot on sauté setting, cook onion, celery and garlic in butter until slightly softened, about 2 minutes.

- Add kale, cauliflower, stock and balsamic vinegar to pot and season to taste with salt and pepper.

- Secure pot lid, close pressure valve and cook on high for 3 minutes. Let pressure release naturally.

- Slowly pour cream into soup, stirring constantly. Mash some of the cauliflower if desired for a thicker consistency.

- Ladle soup into bowls and garnish with Parmesan cheese to serve. Enjoy!

Per Serving: Calories: 267; Total Fat: 15g; Saturated Fat: 10g; Protein: 10; Carbs: 24g; Fiber: 7g; Sugar: 4g

Mashed Cauliflower

Serves: 4 / Preparation time: 5 minutes / Cooking time: 15 minutes

For keto diet followers, mashed cauliflower is a common substitute for mashed potatoes. Mashed cauliflower is delicious served alongside any main-dish meat. Create a quick meal-in-a-bowl by topping servings of mashed cauliflower with chopped ham and Swiss cheese, or chicken and broccoli, or any meats, vegetables and cheeses of your choice.

1 cup chicken, beef or vegetable stock

Salt and freshly ground black pepper, to taste

1 large head cauliflower (about 3 pounds), cut into large chunks

2 tablespoons butter

2 tablespoons heavy cream

- Pour stock into Instant Pot. Place cauliflower in steamer basket and set in pot. Season cauliflower to taste with salt and pepper.

- Secure pot lid, close pressure valve and cook on steam setting for 6 minutes. When cooking time ends, let pressure release naturally.

- Remove cauliflower from steamer basket to a large bowl and add butter and heavy cream. Mash cauliflower to desired consistency with a fork, potato ricer, or immersion blender.

- Season cauliflower to taste with salt and pepper to serve. Enjoy!

Per Serving: Calories: 128; Total Fat: 8g; Saturated Fat: 5g; Protein: 4g; Carbs: 11g; Fiber: 5g; Sugar: 5g

Broccoli Cheese Soup

Serves: 8 / Preparation time: 15 minutes / Cooking time: 10 minutes

This recipe can be doubled if you're serving a crowd. You can save leftovers, if there are any, for up to 3 days in the refrigerator. If you can't find Colby cheese, you can substitute mild or medium cheddar.

2 tablespoons butter

1 medium onion, diced

4 cloves garlic, peeled and minced

4 cups chicken stock

4 cups broccoli florets

1 cup heavy cream

8 ounces Colby cheese, shredded

- In Instant Pot on sauté setting, melt butter and cook onion and garlic until translucent, about 5 minutes. Add broccoli and chicken stock to pot and season to taste with salt and pepper.

- Secure pot lid, close pressure valve and cook on high setting for 5 minutes. When cooking time ends, carefully turn venting knob from sealing to venting position for a quick pressure release.

- Add heavy cream and Colby cheese to soup and stir until cheese is melted. Season soup to taste with salt and pepper, serve and enjoy!

Per Serving: Calories: 268; Total Fat: 22g; Saturated Fat: 15g; Protein: 8g; Carbs: 5g; Fiber: 4g; Sugar: 2g

Warm Broccoli Salad

Serves: 4 / Preparation time: 15 minutes / Cooking time: 8 minutes

You can substitute a 12-ounce bag of broccoli slaw mix for the head of broccoli in this recipe, but beware of the extra carbs added if the mix contains carrots. If you have red cabbage on hand, you can shred some and add it to the pot with the broccoli for some added color.

1 head broccoli (about 1 pound)

1 small red onion, sliced

2 tablespoons coconut oil

½ teaspoon dried ginger

1 lime, zested and juiced

Salt and freshly ground black pepper, to taste

1 cup unflavored whole-milk yogurt

2 tablespoons finely chopped roasted peanuts

- Peel broccoli stalks if necessary and cut into julienne strips. Cut broccoli florets into bite-size pieces. Set broccoli aside.

- In Instant Pot on sauté setting, melt coconut oil and cook onion until translucent, about 5 minutes.

- Add broccoli, ginger and lime zest to pot, season to taste with salt and pepper and mix well.

- Secure pot lid, close pressure valve and cook on manual setting until broccoli is crisp-tender, about 3 minutes. Carefully turn venting knob from sealing to venting position for a quick pressure release.

- Stir yogurt and lime juice into broccoli mixture and sprinkle with chopped peanuts to serve. Enjoy!

Per Serving: Calories: 193; Total Fat: 11g; Saturated Fat: 8g; Protein: 7g; Carbs: 17g; Fiber: 5g; Sugar: 8g

Steamed Kale with Bacon

Serves: 4 / Preparation time: 10 minutes / Cooking time: 10 minutes

This savory side dish comes together in a snap. Turn it into a main dish by stirring in about 2 cups of fully cooked diced ham or chicken with the kale at the end.

1 bunch kale, about 8 cups chopped

1 tablespoon butter

1 onion, diced

4 slices bacon, diced

Salt and fresh coarsely ground black pepper, to taste

- Pour 1 cup water into Instant Pot and set steamer basket in pot. Place kale in steamer basket.

- Secure pot lid, close pressure valve and cook on steam setting for 5 minutes. When cooking time ends, let pressure release naturally. Remove steamer basket from pot and drain pot.

- In Instant Pot on sauté setting, melt butter and cook onion and bacon until onion is translucent and bacon is crisped, about 5 minutes.

- Stir kale into onion mixture and season to taste with salt and pepper. Serve with a slotted spoon and enjoy!

Per Serving: Calories: 117; Total Fat: 5g; Saturated Fat: 3g; Protein: 6g; Carbs: 11g; Fiber: 4g; Sugar: 0g

Broccoli Cauliflower Soup

Serves: 6 / Preparation time: 10 minutes / Cooking time: 30 minutes

Starting with frozen broccoli and cauliflower makes this soup easy to prepare at a moment's notice. Pair this soup with a leafy green salad with vinegar and oil dressing for a perfect cool-weather lunch.

1 tablespoon butter

3 stalks celery, trimmed and diced

1 small onion, diced

3 cloves garlic, peeled and minced

1 package (10 ounces) frozen broccoli

1 package (10 ounces) frozen cauliflower

4 cups chicken stock

1 package (3 ounces) cream cheese, softened

¼ teaspoon ground nutmeg

6 ounces sharp cheddar cheese, shredded

Salt and freshly ground black pepper, to taste

- In Instant Pot on sauté setting, melt butter and cook celery, onion and garlic until translucent, about 5 minutes.

- Add broccoli, cauliflower, chicken stock, cream cheese and nutmeg to pot and season to taste with salt and pepper.

- Secure pot lid, close pressure valve and cook on high setting for 30 minutes. When cooking time ends, let pressure release naturally.

- For chunky soup, serve immediately; otherwise puree soup with an immersion blender to desired texture. Garnish servings of soup with grated cheese and enjoy!

Per Serving: Calories: 228; Total Fat: 16g; Saturated Fat: 9g; Protein: 9g; Carbs: 7g; Fiber: 5g; Sugar: 2g

Poultry

Turkey Thighs

Serves: 6 / Preparation time: 10 minutes / Cooking time: 40 minutes

Chicken or other turkey parts can be substituted for the turkey thighs, but you may have to adjust the cooking time. After cooking, you can strain the juices left in the pot and make a savory gravy using the thickener of your choice.

1 teaspoon rubbed sage

1 teaspoon dried rosemary, crushed

1 teaspoon thyme

Salt and freshly ground pepper, to taste

3 turkey thighs, skin removed

2 tablespoons olive oil

1 onion, peeled and diced

4 cloves garlic, peeled and minced

2 cups chicken stock

- Combine sage, rosemary and thyme, rub over turkey thighs and season to taste with salt and pepper.

- In Instant Pot on sauté setting, brown thighs in 1 tablespoon olive oil on all sides.

- Remove thighs from pot and set aside. Add remaining olive oil to pot and sauté onion and garlic until translucent, about 5 minutes. Return thighs to pot, add stock and season to taste with salt and pepper.

- Secure pot lid, close pressure valve and cook on high setting until done, about 30 minutes. When cooking time ends, let pressure release naturally. Cut meat from bones into slices to serve. Enjoy!

Per Serving: Calories: 321; Total Fat: 21g; Saturated Fat: 5g; Protein: 310g; Carbs: 3g; Fiber: 2g; Sugar: 0g

Pulled Chicken Taco Salad

Serves: 4 / Preparation time: 15 minutes / Cooking time: 15 minutes

If your chicken breasts are frozen, you don't need to thaw them before cooking. Just add to the pot when the recipe indicates and increase cooking time for 2-4 minutes until done. Omitting the tomatoes from the salads will cut out 7 grams of carbs and 6 grams of sugar.

1 tablespoon olive oil

1 large onion, julienned

1 bell pepper, julienned

4 cloves garlic, peeled and minced

4 boneless, skinless chicken breasts

½ cup water

1 tablespoon chili powder

1 tablespoon cumin

½ tablespoon ancho chili powder

½ teaspoon dried oregano

¼ teaspoon cayenne pepper

Salt and freshly ground black pepper, to taste

1 small head green leaf lettuce, torn into bite-size pieces (about 8 cups total)

4 ounces cojack cheese, shredded

4 Roma tomatoes, chopped

4 tablespoons sour cream

1 avocado, pitted and sliced

- Heat oil in Instant Pot on sauté setting and cook onion, bell pepper and garlic until softened, about 5 minutes.

- Mix chili powder, cumin, ancho chili powder, oregano and cayenne pepper. Add chicken and water to pot and sprinkle spice mixture over chicken. Season chicken to taste with salt and pepper and stir lightly to coat chicken with spice mixture.

- Secure pot lid, close pressure valve and cook on high setting until done, about 10 minutes. When cooking time ends, allow pressure to release naturally. Remove chicken from pot and shred with a fork. Mix juices from pot into shredded chicken.

- Divide lettuce among 4 serving plates and top with shredded cheese, tomatoes and about 1 tablespoon sour cream. Garnish salads with avocado slices.

- Serve chicken with a slotted spoon on top of the salads or alongside as desired. Enjoy!

Per Serving: Calories: 597; Total Fat: 34; Saturated Fat: 10g; Protein: 53g; Carbs: 18g; Fiber: 7g; Sugar: 9g

Chicken Vindaloo

Serves: 4 / Preparation time: 15 minutes / Cooking time: 15 minutes

Serve chicken vindaloo over riced cauliflower (see recipe in Vegetables section). Easily crank up the heat of this dish by adding more cayenne pepper—use up to 2 teaspoons. Vindaloo is traditionally quite spicy!

1 teaspoon ground ginger

1 teaspoon ground coriander

1 teaspoon paprika

1 teaspoon cumin

½ teaspoon turmeric

½ teaspoon cinnamon

½ teaspoon cayenne pepper

½ teaspoon cardamom

1/8 teaspoon ground cloves

1 onion, finely diced

4 cloves garlic, peeled and minced

1 tablespoon olive oil

½ cup water

1 tablespoon red wine vinegar

Salt and freshly ground black pepper, to taste

1 pound boneless skinless chicken thighs, cut into large chunks

- In a small bowl, combine ginger, coriander, paprika, cumin, turmeric, cinnamon, cayenne pepper, cardamom and cloves and set aside.

- In Instant Pot on sauté setting, cook onion and garlic in oil until softened, about 5 minutes. Add spice mixture to pot and cook for about 1 minute, stirring constantly.

- Add water and vinegar to pot and mix well. Thoroughly scrape bottom of pot to loosen any spices or browned bits.

- Add chicken to pot and stir to coat. Secure pot lid, close pressure valve and cook at high pressure until done, about 5 minutes. When cooking time ends, allow pressure to release naturally.

- If desired, remove chicken and boil sauce down on sauté setting to reduce to desired consistency. Serve and enjoy!

Per Serving: Calories: 218; Total Fat: 13g; Saturated Fat: 3g; Protein: 15g; Carbs: 4g; Fiber: 2g; Sugar: 0g

Rosemary Chicken

Serves: 4 / Preparation time: 10 minutes / Cooking time: 35 minutes

Use a large pair of tongs and a large spatula to help set the whole chicken in the Instant Pot and later to turn it over. Serve the whole chicken carved as a main dish with your favorite sides, or shred or dice it to use in your favorite recipes that call for cooked chicken.

1 whole roasting chicken (about 4 pounds), giblets removed

2 tablespoons peanut oil

Salt and freshly ground black pepper, to taste

2 tablespoons dried rosemary, divided

1 onion, quartered

2 stalks celery, trimmed and cut into 2-inch pieces

1 cup chicken stock

- Rinse chicken and pat dry. Brush oil over outside of chicken and inside body cavity and season to taste with salt and pepper. Crush half of the dried rosemary and sprinkle inside chicken. Place onion and celery inside chicken and tie drumsticks together with kitchen twine.

- Set Instant Pot to sauté setting. Carefully set chicken in pot breast-side down and cook until skin is browned, 3-4 minutes. Carefully turn chicken breast-side up and cook until skin is browned, about 3-4 more minutes.

- Remove chicken from pot, pour stock into pot and set trivet in pot. Place chicken breast-side up on trivet and tuck in wings. Sprinkle remaining crushed rosemary over chicken and season to taste with salt and pepper.

- Secure pot lid, close pressure valve and cook at high pressure until done, about 25 minutes. When cooking time ends, allow pressure to release naturally.

- Remove chicken from pot to a serving platter and let rest for about 5 minutes. Remove kitchen twine from drumsticks and remove onion and celery from cavity. Carve chicken as desired and baste with cooking juices, if desired. Serve and enjoy!

Per Serving: Calories: 276; Total Fat: 7g; Saturated Fat: 0g; Protein: 51g; Carbs: 0g; Fiber: 0g; Sugar: 0g

Shredded Chicken Wraps

Serves: 6 / Preparation time: 15 minutes / Cooking time: 5 minutes

If your chicken breasts are frozen, you don't need to thaw them before beginning this simple recipe. Just add 5 minutes to the cooking time. You can easily change up the ethnic flair of these wraps by swapping out the spices. Try using curry powder, or paprika, or an Italian herb blend in place of the chili powder and cumin.

3 boneless, skinless chicken breasts

Salt and freshly ground black pepper, to taste

½ cup chicken broth

½ teaspoon chili powder

½ teaspoon ground cumin

12 large leaves romaine lettuce

- Season chicken breasts to taste with salt and pepper and place in Instant Pot.

- Secure pot lid, close pressure valve and cook on high setting until done, about 5 minutes. When cooking time ends, allow pressure to release naturally.

- Remove chicken breasts to a large bowl and shred with forks. Mix chili powder and cumin into chicken, adding leftover broth from the pot if the chicken mixture is too dry.

- Layer pairs of lettuce leaves together, top with chicken and roll up to serve. Enjoy!

Per Serving: Calories: 179; Total Fat: 6g; Saturated Fat: 2g; Protein: 25g; Carbs: 3g; Fiber: 2g; Sugar: 1g

Bacon-Wrapped Stuffed Chicken Breasts

Serves: 6 / Preparation time: 20 minutes / Cooking time: 10 minutes

If you prefer crispy bacon, arrange the cooked chicken breasts in a broiler-proof pan and broil them for a few minutes, watching carefully to avoid over-browning.

3 boneless skinless chicken breasts

1 package (8 ounces) cream cheese, softened

1 package (10 ounces) frozen spinach

¼ cup chopped red bell pepper

4 cloves garlic, peeled and minced

6 slices bacon

- Using a sharp knife, slice lengthwise into the thicker end of each chicken breast and fold open.

- Mix cream cheese, spinach, red bell pepper and garlic and season to taste with salt and pepper. Spread about ¼ of the cream cheese mixture on each chicken breast.

- Fold each chicken breast over filling and wrap 2 slices of bacon around each chicken breast.

- Pour 1 cup of water into Instant Pot , place trivet in pot and set chicken breasts on trivet. Secure pot lid, close pressure valve and cook on manual setting until done, about 10 minutes. When cooking time ends, allow pressure to release naturally.

- Let chicken breasts rest for about 5 minutes before cutting into slices to serve. Enjoy!

Per Serving: Calories: 365; Total Fat: 25g; Saturated Fat: 12g; Protein: 32g; Carbs: 7g; Fiber: 0g; Sugar: 0g

Lemon Chicken

Serves: 4 / Preparation time: 20 minutes / Cooking time: 10 minutes

Serve this saucy chicken over riced cauliflower for a complete meal. Change up the flavor by using oranges or lime in place of the lemon in this recipe, or use a combination of all three.

2 large boneless skinless chicken breasts, cut into bite-size pieces

2 tablespoons coconut oil

4 cloves garlic, peeled and minced

1 cup chicken stock

2 lemons, zested and juiced

2 tablespoons soy sauce

Salt and freshly ground black pepper, to taste

1 tablespoon arrowroot flour

1 tablespoon water

- In Instant Pot on sauté setting, cook chicken and garlic in coconut oil until lightly browned.

- Add chicken stock, lemon zest, lemon juice and soy sauce to pot and season to taste with salt and pepper.

- Secure pot lid, close pressure valve and cook on poultry setting until done, about 7 minutes. When cooking time ends, allow pressure to release naturally.

- Whisk together the arrowroot flour and water and stir into chicken mixture to thicken. Serve and enjoy!

Per Serving: Calories: 256; Total Fat: 13g; Saturated Fat: 8g; Protein: 25g; Carbs: 8g; Fiber: 0g; Sugar: 0g

Turkey Soup

Serves: 4 / Preparation time: 20 minutes / Cooking time: 10 minutes

Any fresh herb could be used as a garnish for this soup, just chop or mince as desired. Or use whole sprigs for a more formal look.

1 onion, diced

1 medium red bell pepper, diced

4 stalks celery, trimmed and diced

2 cloves garlic, peeled and minced

2 tablespoons butter

1 pound boneless skinless turkey thighs

Salt and freshly ground black pepper, to taste

4 cups chicken stock

½ teaspoon dried oregano

½ teaspoon dried basil

½ teaspoon dried thyme

1 large bay leaf

2 small zucchini, diced

1 cup frozen peas

1 tablespoon fresh cilantro, minced

- In Instant Pot on sauté setting, cook onion, bell pepper, celery and garlic in butter until onion is translucent, about 5 minutes. Move onion mixture to sides of pot.

- Season turkey thighs to taste with salt and pepper, add to pot and cook on both sides until lightly browned, 2-3 minutes per side.

- Add chicken stock, oregano, basil, thyme and bay leaf to pot and season soup to taste with salt and pepper.

- Secure pot lid, close pressure valve and cook on high setting for 15 minutes. When cooking time ends, carefully turn venting knob from sealing to venting position for a quick pressure release.

- Remove turkey thighs from pot and dice or shred as desired. Return turkey to pot and add zucchini and peas. Cover pot and let soup stand until zucchini and peas are warmed, about 5 minutes.

- Remove bay leaf from soup. Ladle soup into bowls and garnish with cilantro. Serve and enjoy!

Per Serving: Calories: 259; Total Fat: 11g; Saturated Fat: 8g; Protein: 33g; Carbs: 5g; Fiber: 2g; Sugar: 3g

Curried Chicken Bowls

Serves: 4 / Preparation time: 20 minutes / Cooking time: 25 minutes

Try it with a tikka masala blend instead of curry powder if you prefer a little less heat.

1 large head cauliflower (about 3 pounds), cut into large chunks

½ teaspoon each of salt & ground ginger

1 medium eggplant, peeled and cut into bite-size cubes

½ cup plain whole-milk yogurt

Salt and ground black pepper, to taste

2 tablespoons coconut oil

2 large boneless skinless chicken breasts, cut into bite-size pieces

8 stalks celery, trimmed and diced

1 large onion, sliced

3 tablespoons curry powder

1 can (14 ounces) coconut milk

½ cup chicken stock

1 lime, cut into wedges

- Pour 1 cup of water into Instant Pot. Place cauliflower in steamer basket and set in pot. Secure pot lid, close pressure valve and cook on manual setting for 1 minute. Carefully turn venting knob from sealing to venting position for a quick pressure release.

- Remove cauliflower from steamer basket to a large bowl, sprinkle with salt and mash with a potato masher. Cover cauliflower to keep warm and set aside.

- Sprinkle ginger, salt, and pepper over eggplant, then stir in yogurt and set aside.

- Drain water from Instant Pot and set to sauté. Melt coconut oil and cook chicken, celery and onion for 4 minutes. Sprinkle curry powder over chicken mixture and season with salt and pepper. Stir to coat chicken mixture with spices and sauté for 1 minute.

- Add coconut milk and chicken stock to pot and mix well. Secure pot lid, close pressure valve and cook on poultry setting until done, about 7 minutes. When cooking time ends, carefully turn venting knob from sealing to venting position for a quick pressure release.

- Set Instant Pot to warm, stir eggplant mixture into pot and season with salt and pepper. Cover pot and let stand for 10 minutes, then fluff cauliflower with a fork and spoon into deep bowls. Ladle curry over cauliflower and garnish with lime wedges to serve.

Per Serving: Calories: 438; Total Fat: 21g; Saturated Fat: 18g; Protein: 36g; Carbs: 19g; Fiber: 9g; Sugar: 10g

Whole Turkey

If your turkey is larger or smaller than the 8 pounds specified in the recipe, you'll need to adjust the cooking time. A whole turkey in an Instant Pot should cook for 6 minutes per pound. If you prefer crispy skin on the turkey, you can quickly broil it in the oven for that roasted look: set cooked turkey in a broiler-proof baking pan, baste with melted butter and broil for about 5 minutes. The juices left in the Instant Pot can be strained and thickened into gravy with the thickener of your choice.

1 whole turkey (about 8 pounds), fresh or defrosted, giblets removed

Salt and freshly ground black pepper, to taste

2 medium onions, cut into wedges

4 stalks celery, trimmed and cut into 2-inch pieces

Fresh or dried herbs of choice, if desired

1 cup chicken stock

- Rinse turkey and pat dry inside and out. Season turkey inside and out to taste with salt and pepper.

- Place onions and celery inside turkey cavity and add fresh or dried herbs of choice, if desired. With kitchen twine, tie drumsticks together and secure wings in tucked position.

- Pour chicken stock into Instant Pot , place trivet in pot and set turkey on trivet.

- Secure pot lid, close pressure valve and cook at high pressure until done, about 48 minutes. When cooking time ends, allow pressure to release naturally.

- Remove turkey from pot to a serving platter and let rest for about 10 minutes. Remove kitchen twine from turkey and remove onion and celery from cavity. Carve turkey as desired and baste with cooking juices, if desired. Serve and enjoy!

Per Serving: Calories: 236; Total Fat: 11g; Saturated Fat: 3g; Protein: 32g; Carbs: 0g; Fiber: 0g; Sugar: 0g

Seafood

Fish Chowder

Serves: 4 / Preparation time: 10 minutes / Cooking time: 20 minutes

Red bell pepper adds brightness and flavor to this comforting soup. Individual servings could be topped with grated cheese and sour cream if desired. Cod, haddock or catfish can be substituted for the tilapia.

1 medium head cauliflower (about 2 pounds), cored and cut into chunks

8 ounces bacon, diced

1 medium onion, diced

1 medium red bell pepper, diced

2 stalks celery, trimmed and diced

2 cloves garlic, peeled and minced

4 cups chicken stock

1 pound tilapia fillets

2 cups plain whole-milk yogurt

1 tablespoon arrowroot flour

Salt and freshly ground black pepper, to taste

- Pour 1 cup water into Instant Pot. Place cauliflower in steamer basket and set in pot. Secure pot lid, close pressure valve and cook cauliflower on high pressure for 5 minutes. When cooking time ends, allow pressure to release naturally. Drain water from pot if necessary. Remove cauliflower from basket and puree with an immersion blender to desired consistency.

- Cook bacon in Instant Pot on sauté setting until crisp. Add onion, bell pepper, celery and garlic and sauté until vegetables are softened, about 3 minutes.

- Add cauliflower, chicken stock and tilapia to pot and season to taste with salt and pepper. Secure pot lid, close pressure valve and cook chowder on high pressure for 5 minutes. When cooking time ends, let pressure release naturally. Set Instant Pot to warm.

- Stir arrowroot flour into yogurt and mix thoroughly. Add yogurt mixture to chowder and stir 2 to 3 minutes until thickened. Break up fish fillets if necessary.

- Serve and enjoy!

Per Serving: Calories: 347; Total Fat: 15g; Saturated Fat: 6g; Protein: 33g; Carbs: 19g; Fiber: 4g; Sugar: 9g

Coconut Lime Catfish Curry

Serves: 4 / Preparation time: 5 minutes / Cooking time: 15 minutes

Red bell peppers brighten the look of this zesty curry, but feel free to use any colors or combination you may have on hand. Serve the curry with Riced Cauliflower for a satisfying meal (see recipe in the Vegetables section).

1 tablespoon coconut oil

1 red bell pepper, seeds and ribs removed, coarsely chopped

1 large onion, coarsely chopped

2 cloves garlic, peeled and minced

3 tablespoons curry powder

1 can (15 ounces) unsweetened coconut milk

1 small lime, zested and juiced

1 pound catfish fillets, rinsed and cut into bite-size pieces

Salt and freshly ground black pepper, to taste

1 cup cherry tomatoes, chopped and drained

- Melt coconut oil in Instant Pot on sauté setting. Add bell pepper, onion and garlic to pot and sauté, stirring frequently, until softened.

- Add curry powder to pot and sauté for about 1 minute, stirring constantly. Stir coconut milk and lime zest into pot, scraping the bottom of the pot to loosen any browned bits.

- Add catfish pieces to pot, mixing thoroughly to coat pieces with sauce. Season sauce to taste with salt and pepper.

- Secure pot lid, close pressure valve and cook for 5 minutes at low pressure. When cooking time ends, allow pressure to release naturally.

- Drizzle lime juice over curry to serve. Garnish with chopped tomatoes as desired. Enjoy!

Per Serving: Calories: 254; Total Fat: 24g; Saturated Fat: 19g; Protein: 18g; Carbs: 8g; Fiber: 2g; Sugar: 4g

Simple Salmon Fillets

Serves: 4 / Preparation time: 10 minutes / Cooking time: 5 minutes

There's no need to thaw the salmon fillets before cooking in the Instant Pot. They steam up quick, flaky and delicious.

1 package (16 ounces) frozen salmon fillets

12 sprigs fresh dill (or 2 teaspoons dried dill weed)

1 lemon, zested and juiced

Salt and ground black pepper, to taste

- Pour 1 cup of water into Instant Pot and set steamer basket in pot.

- Arrange salmon fillets in steamer basket. Place 2 sprigs of dill on each fillet, sprinkle with lemon juice and lemon zest and season to taste with salt and pepper.

- Secure pot lid, close pressure valve and cook on manual setting for 5 minutes. Carefully turn venting knob from sealing to venting position for a quick pressure release.

- Dot salmon fillets with butter and serve immediately. Enjoy!

Per Serving: Calories: 120; Total Fat: 4g; Saturated Fat: 0g; Protein: 21g; Carbs: 0g; Fiber: 0g; Sugar: 0g

Shrimp Scampi

Serves: 4 / Preparation time: 20 minutes / Cooking time: 10 minutes

Like this recipe, traditional shrimp scampi includes white wine. If desired, you can substitute chicken stock for the wine and cut about 4 grams of carbs from each serving.

1 tablespoon butter

1 tablespoon olive oil

4 cloves garlic, peeled and minced

½ teaspoon red pepper flakes

1 pound frozen large shrimp, peeled and deveined

1 cup white wine

½ teaspoon paprika

Salt and freshly ground black pepper, to taste

½ cup plain yogurt

½ cup finely grated Parmesan cheese

½ lemon, zested in strips and juiced

Parsley sprigs, for garnish

- In Instant Pot on sauté setting, mix butter and olive oil until butter is melted. Add garlic and red pepper flakes and sauté until garlic is lightly browned, 1-2 minutes.

- Add shrimp, chicken stock and paprika to pot and season to taste with salt and pepper. Secure pot lid, close pressure valve and cook for 2 minutes on high pressure.

- When cooking time ends, carefully turn valve from sealing to venting position for a quick pressure release.

- Set Instant Pot to sauté, add yogurt and Parmesan cheese to shrimp mixture and stir until cheese is melted.

- Drizzle lemon juice over shrimp scampi and garnish with lemon zest strips and parsley sprigs to serve. Enjoy!

Per Serving: Calories: 403; Total Fat: 28g; Saturated Fat: 10g; Protein: 36g; Carbs: 8g; Fiber: 8g; Sugar: 3g

Teriyaki Salmon

Serves: 4 / Preparation time: 10 minutes, plus ½-2 hours for marinating / Cooking time: 15 minutes

For a delicious lunch, flake the cooked salmon and make wraps with leaves of Romaine lettuce. Or serve the fillets whole with cucumber spears alongside for a tasty dinner. Either way, this easy homemade version of teriyaki sauce will guarantee you'll never go back to the bottled!

¼ cup soy sauce

¼ cup water

¼ cup mirin, sake or sherry

1 tablespoon sesame oil

4 cloves garlic, peeled and minced

1 lime, zested and juiced

2 tablespoons xylitol (or sweetener of choice)

1 tablespoon freshly grated ginger

4 green onions, minced

2 teaspoons fish sauce

1 tablespoon sesame seeds

1 teaspoon blackstrap molasses

Salt, freshly ground black pepper and cayenne pepper, to taste

1 pound thick salmon fillets

1 tablespoon arrowroot flour

2 tablespoons water

- For the marinade, mix soy sauce, water, mirin, sesame oil, garlic, lime juice, lime zest, xylitol, ginger, half of the green onions (set remaining onions aside for garnish), fish sauce, sesame seeds and molasses and season to taste with salt, black pepper and cayenne pepper.

- Place salmon fillets in 2 pans that will fit inside Instant Pot. Pour about ¼ of the marinade over salmon in each pan. Set remaining marinade aside.

- Cover salmon and refrigerate for 30 minutes to 2 hours.

- To cook salmon, pour 1 cup water into Instant Pot and set trivet in pot. Set one pan of salmon on trivet and set other pan across the top of first pan in an X pattern. Secure pot lid, close pressure valve and cook for 8 minutes on high pressure.

- When cooking time ends, carefully turn venting knob from sealing to venting position for a quick pressure release. Remove salmon from pot and cover it with foil to keep it warm.

- Drain water from pot and set pot to sauté. Mix arrowroot flour into water and whisk in pot with remaining marinade. Simmer for 1-2 minutes until sauce reaches desired consistency.
- Drizzle sauce over salmon fillets and garnish with green onions to serve. Enjoy!

Per Serving: Calories: 268; Total Fat: 9g; Saturated Fat: 2g; Protein: 25g; Carbs: 12g; Fiber: 0g; Sugar: 5g

Mediterranean Cod

Serves: 6 / Preparation time: 15 minutes / Cooking time: 15-18 minutes

You can use fresh or frozen cod fillets in this recipe; the different cooking times are noted. If you can't find Kalamata olives, you can substitute stuffed green olives or pitted black olives. Shredded cabbage with a zesty vinegar and oil dressing would make a delicious side dish for this cod.

2 tablespoons olive oil

1 red onion, julienned

1 can (28 ounces) diced tomatoes

1 lemon, zested and juiced

1 teaspoon dried oregano

½ teaspoon dried basil

½ teaspoon dried thyme

Salt and freshly ground black pepper, to taste

1-½ pounds fresh or frozen cod fillets

6 ounces feta cheese, crumbled

12 Kalamata olives, pitted and sliced

- Heat olive oil in Instant Pot on sauté setting. Add onion and cook until softened, 1-2 minutes, stirring constantly.

- Add undrained tomatoes, lemon zest, lemon juice, oregano, basil and thyme to pot and season to taste with salt and pepper. Mix sauce thoroughly and cook for about 10 minutes, stirring occasionally.

- Place cod fillets in pot and stir lightly to cover with sauce. Secure pot lid, close pressure valve and cook on high pressure for 5 minutes if using frozen cod, 3 minutes if using fresh cod.

- When cooking time ends, carefully turn venting knob from sealing to venting position for a quick pressure release.

- Ladle cod fillets and sauce onto plates. Garnish with feta cheese and Kalamata olives to serve. Enjoy!

Per Serving: Calories: 288; Total Fat: 15g; Saturated Fat: 5g; Protein: 24g; Carbs: 11g; Fiber: 2g; Sugar: 7g

Ginger Scallion Tilapia

Serves: 4 / Preparation time: 15 minutes, plus 20-30 minutes for marinating / Cooking time: ## minutes

This recipe is adapted for the Instant Pot from a Chinese classic. You can substitute any firm white fish for the tilapia. If you don't like the texture of sesame seeds, you can instead stir about ½ teaspoon sesame oil into the sauce just before serving.

4 tablespoons soy sauce

2 tablespoons dry white wine

4 cloves garlic, peeled and minced

4 teaspoons natural creamy peanut butter

1 teaspoon white wine vinegar

1 teaspoon minced ginger

1 pound tilapia fillets

6 scallions, julienned

1 knob ginger (about 1-1/2" long), julienned

1 tablespoon peanut oil

1 tablespoon sesame seeds

- For the marinade, whisk soy sauce, white wine, garlic, peanut butter, vinegar and ginger. Place tilapia fillets in a shallow dish, pour marinade over fillets and turn fillets over to coat. Cover dish and refrigerate for 20-30 minutes.

- Pour 2 cups water into Instant Pot and set steamer basket in pot. Remove tilapia fillets from marinade, reserving the marinade. Secure pot lid, close pressure valve and cook on low pressure for 2 minutes. When cooking time ends, carefully turn venting knob from sealing to venting position for a quick pressure release.

- Remove steamer basket from pot and drain water from pot. Set pot to sauté and cook scallions and ginger in peanut oil until softened, about 2 minutes. Stir reserved marinade into pot and heat to a boil, stirring frequently.

- Arrange tilapia fillets on plates. Ladle sauce over tilapia and sprinkle with sesame seeds to serve. Enjoy!

Per Serving: Calories: 187; Total Fat: 9g; Saturated Fat: 2g; Protein: 22g; Carbs: 3 g; Fiber: 0g; Sugar: 0g

Creole Jambalaya

Serves: 4 / Preparation time: 15 minutes / Cooking time: 30 minutes

Traditional jambalaya is cooked with rice, which has been omitted from this version. Ladle this juicy Cajun-spiced stew over riced cauliflower for a traditional presentation, or serve it like a soup. Add more cayenne pepper to crank up the heat.

3 teaspoons paprika

2 teaspoon dried thyme

2 teaspoon dried oregano

1 teaspoon cayenne pepper, or to taste

1 teaspoon freshly ground black pepper

½ teaspoon red pepper flakes

½ teaspoon salt, or to taste

8 ounces Andouille or kielbasa sausage, cut into ½" slices

1 tablespoon olive oil

8 ounces boneless skinless chicken thighs, cut into 1" chunks

1 pound fresh or frozen medium shrimp, peeled and deveined

1 onion, diced

1 green bell pepper, diced

4 stalks celery, trimmed and diced

4 cloves garlic, peeled and minced

1 can (14.5 ounces) diced tomatoes, undrained

1 cup chicken stock

1 teaspoon Worcestershire sauce

2 bay leaves

1 lemon, juiced

Fresh parsley sprigs for garnish, if desired

- Mix paprika, thyme, oregano, cayenne pepper, black pepper, red pepper flakes and salt and set aside.

- In Instant Pot on sauté setting, cook sausage in oil until browned, about 5 minutes. Remove sausage from pot with a slotted spoon and set aside.

- Add more oil to pot if necessary and cook chicken until browned, about 5 minutes. Remove chicken from pot with a slotted spoon and set aside.

- Sauté shrimp in pot very briefly, for just a few seconds. Remove shrimp from pot with a slotted spoon and set aside.

- Cook onion, bell pepper, celery and garlic in pot until onion is translucent, about 3-4 minutes. Add spice mixture to pot and stir to coat. Add tomatoes, chicken stock, bay leaves, Worcestershire sauce and reserved sausage and chicken to pot and mix thoroughly. Secure pot lid, close pressure valve and cook on high pressure for 7 minutes.

- When cooking time ends, carefully turn venting knob from sealing to venting position for a quick pressure release and gently stir shrimp and lemon juice into pot. Replace lid on pot and let stand until shrimp is heated through, about 10 minutes.

- Ladle servings of jambalaya into shallow bowls and garnish with parsley sprigs. Serve and enjoy!

Per Serving: Calories: 341; Total Fat: 17g; Saturated Fat: 6g; Protein: 35g; Carbs: 6g; Fiber: 0g; Sugar: 2g

Steamed Lobster Tails

Serves: 4 / Preparation time: 10 minutes / Cooking time: 4 minutes

These versatile lobster tails can be served simply with lemon juice, salt and pepper as instructed in this recipe. Or, whip up some garlic butter and drizzle it over the lobster meat for a decadent and tasty treat. Or, chop up the lobster meat and stir it into your favorite lobster salad or bisque recipe. Any way you serve them, they're delicious!

1-1/2 cups chicken broth

1 lemon, zested and juiced

2 pounds fresh raw lobster tails in the shells (about 4 tails)

Large bowl of ice water

Salt and freshly ground black pepper, to taste

- Pour 1-1/2 cups chicken broth into Instant Pot and stir in lemon zest. Place trivet in pot and set lobster tails on trivet with shell sides down. Secure pot lid, close pressure valve and cook on high pressure for 4 minutes.

- When cooking time ends, carefully turn venting knob from sealing to venting position for a quick pressure release. Immediately remove lobster tails from pot and place in ice water so they stop cooking.

- Cut down the center of the underside of the tails with a kitchen shears. Remove meat from shells and arrange on serving plates. Drizzle lemon juice on lobster meat and season to taste with salt and pepper. Serve and enjoy!

Per Serving: Calories: 90; Total Fat: 3g; Saturated Fat: 0g; Protein: 14; Carbs: 0g; Fiber: 0g; Sugar: 0g

Salsa Poached Cod

Serves: 4 / Preparation time: 5 minutes / Cooking time: 5 minutes

Serve this saucy cod over rice or mashed cauliflower. Before cooking, sprinkle cod fillets with cayenne pepper to crank up the spice level.

1 jar (16 ounces) salsa

1 package (16 ounces) frozen cod fillets, thawed

1 teaspoon chili powder

Salt and freshly ground black pepper, to taste

- Pour salsa into Instant Pot. Rub chili powder into cod fillets and season to taste with salt and pepper. Place cod fillets into pot and stir lightly to coat with salsa.

- Secure pot lid, close pressure valve and cook on manual setting for 5 minutes.

- When cooking time ends, carefully turn venting knob from sealing to venting position for a quick pressure release.

- Spoon salsa from pot over cod fillets to serve. Enjoy!

Per Serving: Calories: 188; Total Fat: 4g; Saturated Fat: 1g; Protein: 26g; Carbs: 10g; Fiber: 2g; Sugar: 6g

Beef

Stuffed Bell Peppers

Serves: 6 / Preparation time: 15 minutes / Cooking time: 15 minutes

With basil, oregano and two kinds of cheese, these stuffed peppers have an Italian flair. You could substitute ground turkey or Italian sausage for the beef, or combine whatever you have on hand. Use crushed tomatoes instead of tomato sauce if you prefer the texture.

6 bell peppers

1 pound ground beef

1 onion, chopped

1 egg, beaten

1 cup grated mozzarella cheese, divided

2 tablespoons grated Parmesan cheese, divided

1 can (15 ounces) tomato sauce

2 cloves garlic, minced

1 teaspoon dried basil

1 teaspoon dried oregano

Salt and freshly ground black pepper, to taste

- Cut tops from peppers and remove seeds and ribs, leaving peppers intact. Poke holes on the bottoms of the peppers.

- Place ground beef, onion, egg, half of the mozzarella cheese, half of the Parmesan cheese, garlic, basil, and oregano in a mixing bowl, season with salt and pepper and mix thoroughly. Stuff peppers with meat mixture.

- Pour half of the tomato sauce and ½ cup water into Instant Pot. Set trivet in place, set stuffed peppers on trivet and pour remaining tomato sauce over peppers.

- Secure pot lid, close pressure valve and cook at high pressure for about 15 minutes until done. When cooking time ends, let pressure release naturally.

- Sprinkle remaining mozzarella cheese and Parmesan cheese over peppers. Replace lid on pot and let stand until cheese melts.

- Drizzle sauce from the bottom of the pot over the peppers to serve. Enjoy!

Per Serving: Calories: 330; Total Fat: 19g; Saturated Fat: 7g; Protein: 22g; Carbs: 18g; Fiber: 2g; Sugar: 12g

Bacon Cheeseburger Casserole

Serves: 6 / Preparation time: 15 minutes / Cooking time: 30 minutes

This keto casserole is a crowd-pleaser. Family or friends not following a keto diet can be served French fries, rolls or pickles on the side to go along with the cheeseburger theme. Change up the flavor by using sharp cheddar, Colby or cojack cheese in place of the mild cheddar cheese.

1 pound ground beef

2 tablespoons chopped onion

2 cloves garlic, peeled and minced

½ pound bacon, cooked and crumbled

4 eggs, beaten

8 ounces mild cheddar cheese, grated

1 can (6 ounces) tomato paste

½ cup plain whole-milk yogurt

Salt and freshly ground black pepper, to taste

- Mix ground beef, onion and garlic in Instant Pot and season to taste with salt and pepper. Cook on sauté setting, stirring occasionally, until beef is mostly browned. Secure pot lid, close pressure valve and cook at high pressure for 10 minutes. Carefully turn venting knob from sealing to venting position for a quick pressure release.

- Open lid and, if necessary, cook on sauté setting to boil off excess liquid.

- Add bacon to beef mixture and stir to combine.

- Whisk together eggs, tomato paste, yogurt and half of the cheddar cheese and season to taste with salt and pepper. Stir egg mixture into beef mixture and sprinkle with remaining cheese.

- Secure pot lid, close pressure valve and cook at high pressure for about 10 minutes until done. When cooking time ends, let pressure release naturally.

- Serve and enjoy!

Per Serving: Calories: 471; Total Fat: 32g; Saturated Fat: 12g; Protein: 31g; Carbs: 3g; Fiber: 2g; Sugar: 4g

Chunky Steak Chili

Serves: 4 / Preparation time: 15 minutes / Cooking time: 35 minutes

Individual servings of this chili can be garnished with sour cream, sliced pitted black olives, avocado slices or grated cheese. You may be surprised to see cocoa powder on the ingredients list. It adds richness and depth to this chili's flavor.

1 tablespoon chili powder

1 tablespoon ground cumin

1 teaspoon unsweetened cocoa powder

1 teaspoon paprika

1 teaspoon ancho chili powder

1 teaspoon dried oregano

¼ teaspoon cayenne pepper

1 pound round steak, trimmed and cut into 1-inch cubes

1 onion, coarsely diced

4 stalks celery, trimmed and diced

4 cloves garlic, peeled and minced

1 cup beef stock

1 can (6 ounces) tomato paste

1 can (28 ounces) crushed tomatoes

Salt and freshly ground black pepper, to taste

- Mix first 7 ingredients (all the spices) in a bowl and set aside.
- In Instant Pot on sauté setting, cook round steak cubes with half of the spices until meat is browned on all sides. Add onion, celery, garlic, beef stock and tomato paste to pot, season to taste with salt and pepper and mix well.
- Without stirring, add crushed tomatoes to pot. *Do not mix.*
- Secure pot lid, close pressure valve and cook at high pressure for about 12 minutes. When cooking time ends, let pressure release naturally.
- Add remaining spices and mix well. Set pot to sauté, place lid on pot slightly ajar and let chili simmer until reduced to desired consistency, up to about 10 minutes.
- Garnish as desired to serve and enjoy!

Per Serving (calculated without optional garnishes): Calories: 255; Total Fat: 9g; Saturated Fat: 4g; Protein: 31g; Carbs: 21g; Fiber: 7g; Sugar: 11g

Taco Bowls

Serves: 6 / Preparation time: 10 minutes / Cooking time: 20 minutes

These bowls can serve as a versatile base for popular taco fillings—set up a taco bar with grated cheese, sour cream, diced tomatoes, shredded lettuce, black olives, salsa, chopped cilantro, guacamole...any or all of your favorites!

1 large head cauliflower (about 3 pounds), cut into large chunks

½ teaspoon salt

1 pound ground beef

1 small onion, finely diced

2 cloves garlic, minced

1 can (28 ounces) crushed tomatoes

2 teaspoons each of cumin and chili powder

1 teaspoon each of unsweetened cocoa powder, and dried oregano

¼ teaspoon cayenne pepper

Salt and freshly ground black pepper, to taste

1 avocado, pitted and sliced

- Pour 1 cup of water into Instant Pot. Place cauliflower in steamer basket and set in pot. Secure pot lid, close pressure valve and cook on manual setting for 1 minute. Carefully turn venting knob from sealing to venting position for a quick pressure release.

- Remove cauliflower from steamer basket to a large bowl, sprinkle with salt and mash to desired consistency with a potato masher. Cover mash to keep warm and set aside.

- Drain water from Instant Pot and set pot to sauté. Crumble ground beef into pot, add onion and cook until lightly browned, 3-4 minutes. Stir garlic into beef mixture and cook for about 1 minute. If necessary, drain fat from beef mixture.

- Add crushed tomatoes, chili powder, cumin, cocoa powder, oregano and cayenne pepper to pot, season to taste with salt and pepper and mix well.

- Secure pot lid, close pressure valve and cook at high pressure for 8 minutes, then carefully turn venting knob from sealing to venting position for a quick pressure release.

- Fluff cauliflower with a fork and scoop into 6 deep bowls. Ladle taco filling over cauliflower and garnish with avocado slices to serve. Enjoy!

Per Serving: Calories: 325; Total Fat: 21g; Saturated Fat: 6g; Protein: 18g; Carbs: 16g; Fiber: 8g; Sugar: 6g

Creamy Beef Stroganoff

Serves: 4 / Preparation time: 5 minutes / Cooking time: 30 minutes

Serve this creamy stroganoff over "zoodles" (zucchini noodles). To make zoodles, cut zucchini into strips or curls with a spiralizer, mandoline or vegetable peeler. Zoodles don't need to be cooked; just microwave them on high in 30-second intervals until al dente.

1 pound beef stew meat

1 onion, julienned

4 cloves garlic, peeled and minced

1 tablespoon olive oil

2 cups (about 4 ounces) sliced fresh mushrooms

1 cup beef stock or water

1 teaspoon Worcestershire sauce

Salt and freshly ground pepper, to taste

½ cup sour cream

1 teaspoon arrowroot flour

1 tablespoon water

- In Instant Pot on sauté setting, cook onion, garlic and stew meat in oil until beef is lightly browned.

- Add mushrooms, stock and Worcestershire sauce to pot and season to taste with salt and pepper.

- Secure pot lid, close pressure valve and cook at high pressure until done, about 20 minutes. When cooking time ends, let pressure release naturally.

- Set pot to sauté and stir in sour cream. Combine arrowroot flour and water until smooth and stir into stroganoff to thicken. Serve and enjoy!

Per Serving: Calories: 361; Total Fat: 13g; Saturated Fat: 7g; Protein: 28g; Carbs: 8g; Fiber: 4g; Sugar: 2g

Lasagna

Serves: 6 / Preparation time: 10 minutes / Cooking time: 20 minutes

Nobody will miss the pasta in this lasagna recipe. Filled with zesty sauce and gooey cheese, it's sure to be a crowd-pleaser.

1 pound lean ground beef

1 onion, diced

6 cloves garlic, peeled and minced

1 can (28 ounces) crushed tomatoes

2 teaspoons Italian herb blend, plus more for garnish

3 small zucchini, cut lengthwise into strips

Salt and freshly ground black pepper, to taste

1 cup ricotta cheese

6 ounces mozzarella cheese, shredded

½ cup finely grated Parmesan cheese

2 eggs, lightly beaten

1 teaspoon dried oregano

6 ounces mozzarella cheese, sliced

- In Instant Pot on sauté setting, cook ground beef, onion and garlic until ground beef is browned, 5-6 minutes. Drain fat if necessary.

- Add crushed tomatoes and herb blend to pot and season to taste with salt and pepper. Remove half of the beef mixture from pot and set aside.

- Arrange half of the zucchini slices over the beef mixture in the pot. Mix ricotta, mozzarella, Parmesan, eggs and oregano and spread over zucchini slices. Arrange remaining zucchini slices over cheese mixture and top with remaining beef mixture.

- Secure pot lid, close pressure valve and cook at high pressure until done, about 10 minutes. When cooking time ends, carefully turn venting knob from sealing to venting position for a quick pressure release.

- Arrange mozzarella slices over lasagna, cover pot and let stand until cheese is melted. Cut lasagna into wedges and sprinkle with Italian herb blend to serve. Enjoy!

Per Serving: Calories: 379; Total Fat: 22; Saturated Fat: 13g; Protein: 35g; Carbs: 15g; Fiber: 1g; Sugar: 7g

Beef Stew

Serves: 4 / Preparation time: 15 minutes / Cooking time: 40 minutes

Leaving potatoes and carrots out of this recipe makes it keto-friendly. Celery, pearl onions and mushrooms round out the hearty, satisfying beef stew.

1 pound lean beef stew meat

Salt and freshly ground black pepper, to taste

2 tablespoons butter

2 cloves garlic, peeled and minced

2 cups beef stock

2 teaspoons Worcestershire sauce

2 teaspoons soy sauce

1 teaspoon paprika

4 stalks celery, trimmed and cut into 1-inch pieces

1 package (14 ounces) frozen pearl onions

8 ounces sliced mushrooms

2 bay leaves

1 tablespoon arrowroot flour

1 tablespoon water

- Season beef with salt and pepper. In Instant Pot on sauté setting, melt butter and cook stew meat until lightly browned on all sides, about 5 minutes. Add garlic to pot and cook until softened, about 2 minutes.

- Add beef stock, Worcestershire sauce, soy sauce and paprika to pot and stir to deglaze pot.

- Add celery, pearl onions, mushrooms and bay leaves to pot, season stew to taste with salt and pepper and mix thoroughly.

- Secure pot lid, close pressure valve and cook at high pressure for about 30 minutes until done. When cooking time ends, let pressure release naturally. Remove bay leaves from stew.

- Whisk arrowroot flour into water and stir into stew to thicken gravy. Serve and enjoy!

Per Serving: Calories: 273; Total Fat: 16g; Saturated Fat: 9g; Protein: 25g; Carbs: 180g; Fiber: 1g; Sugar: 5g

Round Steak with Peppers

Serves: 4 / Preparation time: 15 minutes / Cooking time: 25 minutes

Mix up the colors of bell peppers used in this recipe to brighten up the final dish. Stir a pinch of cinnamon and a pinch of nutmeg into the pot for an interesting flavor twist. If you'd rather not simmer to reduce the sauce, you can whisk 1 tablespoon arrowroot flour into 1 tablespoon water and stir into the sauce to thicken it.

1 pound round steak, cut into strips

Salt and freshly ground black pepper, to taste

2 tablespoons vegetable oil

2 bell peppers, cut into strips

2 cloves garlic, peeled and minced

1 can (28 ounces) diced tomatoes

1 cup beef stock

¼ cup soy sauce

1 teaspoon dried basil

1 teaspoon dried oregano

½ teaspoon dried thyme

½ teaspoon ground ginger

- Season round steak strips with salt and pepper. In Instant Pot on sauté setting, cook strips in oil until lightly browned, about 5 minutes.

- Add bell pepper strips and garlic to pot and cook until slightly softened, 2-3 minutes.

- Add undrained tomatoes, beef stock, soy sauce, basil, oregano, thyme and ginger to pot, season to taste with salt and pepper and mix well.

- Secure pot lid, close pressure valve and cook at stew setting for 15 minutes. When cooking time ends, carefully turn venting knob from sealing to venting position for a quick pressure release.

- On sauté setting, simmer steak and peppers, stirring frequently, to reduce sauce to desired consistency. Serve and enjoy!

Per Serving: Calories: 310; Total Fat: 15g; Saturated Fat: 4g; Protein: 27g; Carbs: 12g; Fiber: 3g; Sugar: 8g

Hearty Spaghetti Sauce

Serves: 4 / Preparation time: 10 minutes / Cooking time: 15 minutes

Serve this savory sauce over riced cauliflower or shredded spaghetti squash. Season the sauce to your taste by substituting your own mixture of dried basil, oregano, thyme and rosemary. If you're using fresh herbs, finely chop them and stir them into the sauce just before serving.

1 pound lean ground beef

1 link Italian sausage, casing removed

1 onion, diced

1 red bell pepper, diced

4 cloves garlic, peeled and minced

Salt and freshly ground black pepper, to taste

1 can (28 ounces) crushed tomatoes

8 ounces fresh mushrooms, sliced

1 tablespoon Italian herb mix

½ teaspoon dried red pepper flakes

½ cup freshly grated Parmesan cheese

- Set Instant Pot to sauté. Crumble ground beef and sausage into pot and add onion, bell pepper and garlic. Season beef mixture to taste with salt and pepper and cook until browned, 5-6 minutes. If necessary, drain fat from pot.

- Add crushed tomatoes, mushrooms, herb mix and red pepper flakes to pot and mix well.

- Secure pot lid, close pressure valve and cook at high pressure for 8 minutes. When cooking time ends, carefully turn venting knob from sealing to venting position for a quick pressure release.

- Transfer sauce to a large bowl and sprinkle with Parmesan cheese to serve. Enjoy!

Per Serving: Calories: 358; Total Fat: 15g; Saturated Fat: 6g; Protein: 37g; Carbs: 17g; Fiber: 4g; Sugar: 8g

Boneless BBQ Beef Ribs

Serves: 4 / Preparation time: 10 minutes / Cooking time: 30 minutes

Serve these zesty ribs with a crispy coleslaw and roasted vegetables for a hearty down-home meal. Save any extra sauce and drizzle it over shredded chicken or pork for delicious wraps.

2 teaspoons onion powder

1 teaspoon garlic powder

1 teaspoon cumin

1 teaspoon chili powder

¼ teaspoon chipotle chili powder

1 pound boneless beef ribs

2 tablespoons peanut oil

4 slices bacon, diced

1 large onion, diced

1 ½ cups beef stock

2 tablespoons red wine vinegar

2 tablespoons tomato paste

1 tablespoon arrowroot flour

1 tablespoon water

- Mix onion powder, garlic powder, cumin, chili powder and chipotle chili powder and rub over ribs. Season ribs with salt and pepper.

- Heat oil in Instant Pot on sauté setting and cook ribs until lightly browned on all sides, about 8 minutes. Remove ribs from pot and set aside.

- Cook bacon in pot until lightly browned. Add onion and cook for 3 more minutes.

- Add stock to pot and mix thoroughly, scraping bottom of pot to loosen browned bits. Stir vinegar and tomato paste into pot and return ribs to pot, stirring lightly to coat ribs.

- Secure pot lid, close pressure valve and cook at high pressure for 20 minutes. When cooking time ends, let pressure release naturally.

- Remove ribs from pot and cover to keep warm. Strain fat from juices in pot and set pot to sauté. Whisk arrowroot flour into water, add to pot and stir until sauce is thickened.

- Turn Instant Pot off, return ribs to pot and stir lightly to coat with sauce. Let ribs stand in sauce for about 10 minutes before serving. Enjoy!

Per Serving: Calories: 374; Total Fat: 31g; Saturated Fat: 11g; Protein: 16g; Carbs: 5g; Fiber: 1g; Sugar: 1g

Pork

Pulled Pork Carnitas

Serves: 8 / Preparation time: 30 minutes / Cooking time: 40 minutes

For a crispy finish, spread the cooked pulled pork on a baking sheet, drizzle with juices from the pot and broil in the oven until browned. Add more cayenne pepper before cooking to turn up the heat. Serving the meat on a corn tostada adds about 10 grams of carbs.

3 pounds pork tenderloin, cut into 2-inch cubes

1 teaspoon salt

½ teaspoon freshly ground pepper

¼ teaspoon cayenne pepper

1 cup chicken stock

4 cloves garlic, peeled and minced

1 orange, juiced and zested

1 lime, juiced and zested

Salt and freshly ground black pepper, to taste

8 ounces sour cream

2 avocados, cut into slices

- Toss pork cubes with salt and pepper to coat. Cook pork in instant pot on sauté setting until browned on all sides.

- Mix chicken stock, garlic, orange juice, orange zest, lime juice and lime zest and pour into pot with pork. Secure pot lid, close pressure valve and cook at high pressure until done, about 30 minutes. When cooking time ends, let pressure release naturally.

- Shred cooked pork with two forks, season with salt and pepper to taste and stir.

- Serve onto plates with a slotted spoon. Dollop servings with sour cream and garnish with avocado slices. Enjoy!

Per Serving: Calories: 381; Total Fat: 22g; Saturated Fat: 8g; Protein: 37g; Carbs: 7g; Fiber: 3g; Sugar: 0g

Baby Back Ribs

Serves: 6 / Preparation time: 10 minutes / Cooking time: 60 minutes

These savory baby back ribs will come out of the instant pot falling-off-the-bone tender. For a smokier flavor, add ¼ teaspoon chipotle chili powder to the rub.

1 teaspoon salt

1 teaspoon paprika

1 teaspoon chili powder

½ teaspoon freshly ground black pepper

½ teaspoon cumin

¼ teaspoon cayenne pepper

2 tablespoons olive oil

3 pounds baby back pork ribs

6 ounces bacon, chopped

1 onion, coarsely chopped

4 cloves garlic, peeled and minced

1-1/2 cups beef or vegetable stock

3 tablespoons tomato paste

1 tablespoon arrowroot flour

1/4 cup water

- Combine salt, paprika, chili powder, black pepper, cumin and cayenne pepper and rub over ribs. Heat 1 tablespoon oil in instant pot on sauté setting and cook half of the ribs until meat is browned on all sides, 4-5 minutes. Repeat with remaining oil and ribs. Remove ribs from pot and set aside.

- Sauté bacon in pot until lightly browned. Stir onion and garlic into pot with bacon and sauté until translucent, 2-3 minutes.

- Add stock and tomato paste to pot, stir to loosen browned bits and return ribs to pot. Secure pot lid, close pressure valve and cook at high pressure until meat is very tender, about 40 minutes. Cook longer if necessary. When cooking time ends, let pressure release naturally.

- Remove ribs to a plate, cover and set aside. Skim fat from juices in pot if necessary. Thoroughly mix arrowroot flour into water and stir into pot juices to thicken. Return ribs to pot and stir gently to coat ribs with sauce. Cover pot and let stand for about 10 minutes, stirring occasionally. Serve and enjoy!

Per Serving: Calories: 427; Total Fat: 27g; Saturated Fat: 10g; Protein: 40g; Carbs: 6g; Fiber: 0g; Sugar: 1g

Ham & Asparagus Soup

Serves: 6 / Preparation time: 20 minutes / Cooking time: 60 minutes

Asparagus is more keto-friendly than the split peas traditionally used in this soup. If you have some extra leftover ham, sprinkle it atop this flavorful soup as a hearty garnish.

1 tablespoon butter

1 onion, diced

4 stalks celery, trimmed and diced

2 cloves garlic, peeled and minced

1 meaty ham bone

4 cups chicken stock

2 pounds asparagus stalks

1 bay leaf

½ teaspoon dried thyme

Salt and ground black pepper, to taste

- Melt butter in instant pot on sauté setting and cook onion, celery and garlic until softened, about 5 minutes.

- Add ham bone and stock to pot and simmer for 3 minutes.

- Peel and trim asparagus stalks as necessary, cut in half and add to pot with thyme. Season soup to taste with salt and pepper.

- Secure pot lid, close pressure valve and cook on soup setting for about 45 minutes. When cooking time ends, let pressure release naturally. Remove ham bone and shred ham with a fork. If desired, blend soup with an immersion blender to desired consistency. Stir ham into soup, serve and enjoy!

Per Serving (calculations based on 3 oz. ham per serving): Calories: 296; Total Fat: 17g; Saturated Fat: 7g; Protein: 22g; Carbs: 10g; Fiber: 3g; Sugar: 3g

Smothered Pork Chops

Serves: 4 / Preparation time: 15 minutes / Cooking time: 25 minutes

With "smothered" in their title, you know these chops are going to be good! Sautéing the pork chops and the onion mixture adds richness to the flavor of this traditional dish. Serve with seasonal vegetables and some mashed cauliflower for a complete, hearty meal.

4 boneless top loin pork chops (about 4 ounces each)

1 teaspoon poultry seasoning

Salt and freshly ground black pepper, to taste

2 tablespoons coconut oil

1 large onion, sliced

4 cloves garlic, peeled and minced

8 ounces fresh sliced mushrooms

1 cup chicken stock

1 teaspoon paprika

1 teaspoon arrowroot flour

½ cup heavy cream

- Rub poultry seasoning into pork chops and season to taste with salt and pepper. Melt 1 tablespoon coconut oil in Instant Pot on sauté setting and cook pork chops until brown on both sides, about 6 minutes. Remove pork chops from pot and set aside.

- Melt remaining coconut oil in pot and sauté onion, garlic and mushrooms until softened and onions are translucent, about 5 minutes.

- Return pork chops to pot and add chicken stock and paprika. Secure pot lid, close pressure valve and cook on meat/stew setting for about 12 minutes. When cooking time ends, let pressure release naturally.

- Move the chops to the edge of the pot. Add cream and arrowroot flour to juices in pot, season to taste with salt and pepper and whisk to thicken the gravy.

- Serve the chops smothered with the gravy. Enjoy!

Per Serving: Calories: 308; Total Fat: 190g; Saturated Fat: 11g; Protein: 25g; Carbs: 4g; Fiber: 2g; Sugar: 0g

Crustless Ham & Swiss Quiche

Serves: 8 / Preparation time: 15 minutes / Cooking time: 30 minutes

Cooked without a crust, this quiche is keto-friendly. For a dash of color, garnish wedges of this savory quiche with bright sprigs of parsley, a dash of chopped fresh chives or a sprinkle of thinly sliced green onion rings.

8 eggs, beaten

1 cup plain whole-milk yogurt

Salt and freshly ground black pepper, to taste

2 cups fully cooked diced ham

1 cup shredded Swiss cheese

- Pour 1 cup water into Instant Pot and set trivet in bottom of pot.

- Whisk together eggs and yogurt and season to taste with salt and pepper.

- Grease a soufflé dish that will fit inside the Instant Pot. Arrange the ham and half of the Swiss cheese in the soufflé dish. Pour egg mixture into soufflé dish and cover dish loosely with aluminum foil. Carefully set soufflé dish on trivet in Instant Pot.

- Secure pot lid, close pressure valve and cook at high pressure for about 30 minutes. When cooking time ends, let pressure release naturally.

- Carefully remove soufflé dish from pot and remove foil from soufflé. Sprinkle remaining Swiss cheese over soufflé. Cover soufflé with foil and let stand 1-2 minutes to allow cheese to melt.

- Cut soufflé into wedges to serve. Enjoy!

Per Serving: Calories: 262; Total Fat: 16g; Saturated Fat: 8g; Protein: 26g; Carbs: 2g; Fiber: 0g; Sugar: 2g

Savory Pork Loin

Serves: 4 / Preparation time: 10 minutes / Cooking time: 30 minutes

This simple recipe yields tender, juicy slices of pork loin. Use the cooking time to roast up some seasonal vegetables for a fit-for-company dinner.

1 boneless pork loin roast (1 pound)

2 cloves garlic, peeled and minced

1 tablespoon dried rosemary, crushed

Salt and freshly ground pepper, to taste

1 cup chicken stock

- Pierce pork loin all over with a fork or tip of a sharp knife. Mix garlic and rosemary and rub over pork loin, pressing mixture into piercings. Season pork loin to taste with salt and pepper.

- Place pork loin in Instant Pot and add chicken stock. Secure pot lid, close pressure valve and cook on stew setting for 30 minutes. When cooking time ends, let pressure release naturally.

- Cut pork loin into slices to serve. Enjoy!

Per Serving: Calories: 162; Total Fat: 6g; Saturated Fat: 2; Protein: 23g; Carbs: 0g; Fiber: 0g; Sugar: 0g

BBQ Boneless Ribs

Serves: 4 / Preparation time: ## minutes / Cooking time: ## minutes

A quick crunchy cabbage or broccoli coleslaw with vinegar and oil dressing would make a perfect accompaniment for these tender, juicy ribs. Or shred the ribs, stir in some of the juices from the pot and wrap the meat in lettuce leaves for a quick sandwich-style lunch.

1 medium onion, sliced

2 cloves garlic, peeled and minced

1 tablespoon butter

1 pound boneless pork ribs

1 teaspoon chili powder

½ teaspoon paprika

¼ teaspoon ground cumin

¼ teaspoon ground chipotle chili pepper

Salt and freshly ground black pepper, to taste

1 can (28 ounces) crushed tomatoes

2 tablespoons lemon juice

1 tablespoon cider vinegar

1 tablespoon soy sauce

- In Instant Pot on sauté setting, cook onion in butter until onion is translucent, about 4 minutes. Add garlic to pot and cook about 1 minute more. Season ribs to taste with salt and pepper, add to pot and sauté until ribs are lightly browned, 2-3 minutes.

- Mix chili powder, paprika, cumin and chipotle Chile pepper and sprinkle over ribs, turning ribs to coat with spices. Sauté ribs for about 1 more minute.

- Add crushed tomatoes, lemon juice, vinegar and soy sauce to pot and stir gently.

- Secure pot lid, close pressure valve and cook on high pressure until done, about 30 minutes. When cooking time ends, let pressure release naturally.

- Serve and enjoy!

Per Serving: Calories: 227; Total Fat: 9g; Saturated Fat: 3g; Protein: 26g; Carbs: 13g; Fiber: 4g; Sugar: 5

Loaded Cauliflower Bowls

Serves: 6 / Preparation time: 15 minutes / Cooking time: 10-12 minutes

You could substitute any cooked meat you may have on hand for the ham in this recipe. The creamy cauliflower mixture would be delicious topped with shredded chicken, pulled pork or crumbled bacon.

1 large head cauliflower (about 3 pounds), cut into large chunks

Salt and freshly ground black pepper, to taste

1 package (3 ounces) cream cheese, cut into 1/2" pieces

2 tablespoons butter, divided

½ small onion, finely diced

12 ounces fully cooked ham, cut into 1/2" cubes

4 ounces mild cheddar cheese, shredded

¼ cup green onions, cut into rings

4 tablespoons sour cream

- Pour 1 cup water into Instant Pot. Place cauliflower in steamer basket and set in pot. Season cauliflower to taste with salt and pepper.

- Secure pot lid, close pressure valve and cook on steam setting for 6 minutes. When cooking time ends, carefully turn venting knob from sealing to venting position for a quick pressure release.

- Remove cauliflower from steamer basket to a large bowl, add cream cheese and 1 tablespoon butter and puree with an immersion blender until smooth. Cover cauliflower mash to keep it warm and set aside.

- Set Instant Pot to sauté, melt butter and cook onion until transparent, 2-3 minutes. Add ham to pot and stir until ham is lightly browned, 2-3 minutes.

- Scoop cauliflower mixture into 6 deep bowls and sprinkle ham mixture and cheese over cauliflower. Garnish bowls with green onions and sour cream to serve. Enjoy!

Per Serving: Calories: 362; Total Fat: 27g; Saturated Fat: 15g; Protein: 20g; Carbs: 6g; Fiber: 3g; Sugar: 1g

Garlic Thyme Pork Shoulder

Serves: 4 / Preparation time: 10 minutes / Cooking time: 45 minutes

If you'd like, at the end of the cooking time, you could strain the juices from the pot and make gravy with the thickener of your choice. You can easily adapt this recipe to your own preferences by using different combinations of spices and cooking liquids.

1 boneless pork shoulder (about 2 pounds)

4 cloves garlic, minced

2 tablespoons peanut oil

Salt and freshly ground black pepper, to taste

1 cup chicken stock

1 teaspoon dried thyme

- Score pork shoulder all over with a sharp knife in a diamond pattern and rub with garlic. Brush peanut oil over pork and season to taste with salt and pepper.

- In Instant Pot on sauté setting, cook pork shoulder, turning frequently until browned on all sides, about 10 minutes total. Sprinkle thyme over pork shoulder and season to taste with salt and pepper, turning pork shoulder to season on all sides.

- Pour 1 cup water into pot, secure pot lid and close pressure valve. Cook pork shoulder at high pressure until done, about 35 minutes. When cooking time ends, allow pressure to release naturally.

- Remove pork shoulder from pot to a serving platter and let rest for about 10 minutes. Cut pork shoulder into thick slices, serve and enjoy!

Per Serving: Calories: 325; Total Fat: 19; Saturated Fat: 8g; Protein: 33g; Carbs: 0g; Fiber: 0g; Sugar: 0g

Smoked Sausage & Cabbage

Serves: 4 / Preparation time: 15 minutes / Cooking time: 8 minutes

To add a burst of color to this dish, cut a red bell pepper into strips and stir into the pot with the onion. For an extra smoky kick, add ¼ to ½ teaspoon smoked paprika with the cabbage.

2 tablespoons butter

1 pound smoked Polish pork sausage links, cut into 1-inch pieces

1 small onion, cut into strips

1 large head cabbage, cored and cut into strips

2 cups chicken stock

Salt and freshly ground black pepper, to taste

- Melt butter in Instant Pot on sauté setting and cook sausage and onion until lightly browned on all sides, about 5 minutes.

- Add cabbage and stock to pot, mix well and season to taste with salt and pepper.

- Secure pot lid and close pressure valve and cook pork high pressure for about 3 minutes. When cooking time ends, carefully turn venting knob from sealing to venting position for a quick pressure release.

- Serve smoked sausage & cabbage with a slotted spoon. Enjoy!

Per Serving: Calories: 310; Total Fat: 28g; Saturated Fat: 11g; Protein: 12g; Carbs: 6g; Fiber: 2g; Sugar: 3g

The "Dirty Dozen" and "Clean 15"

Every year, the Environmental Working Group releases a list of the produce with the most pesticide residue (Dirty Dozen) and a list of the ones with the least chance of having residue (Clean 15). It's based on data from the U.S. Department of Agriculture and reveals that 70% of the 48 types of produce that was tested had residues of at least one type of pesticide. On the thousands of samples, there were 178 different pesticides and pesticide breakdown products. This residue can stay on veggies and fruit even after they are washed and peeled.

All pesticides are toxic to humans, and when there is residue left on our food, it has a negative impact on our health. Consequences can include damage to the nervous system, reproductive system, cancer, a weakened immune system, and more. Women who are pregnant can expose their unborn children to toxins through their diet, and continued exposure to pesticides can affect their development.

This year, pears and potatoes join the Dirty Dozen, while cucumbers and cherry tomatoes were removed. Those two types of produce are not on the Clean 15 list, though, so they're clearly still a risk for pesticide residue. This info can help you choose the best fruits and veggies, as well as which ones you should always try to buy organic.

THE DIRTY DOZEN

Strawberries
Spinach
Nectarines
Apples
Peaches
Celery

Grapes
Pears
Cherries
Tomatoes
Sweet bell peppers
Potatoes

THE CLEAN 15

Sweet corn
Avocados
Pineapples
Cabbage
Onions
Frozen sweet peas
Papayas

Asparagus
Mangoes
Eggplant
Honeydew
Kiwi
Cantaloupe
Cauliflower
Grapefruit

Measurement Conversion Tables

Volume Equivalents (Liquid)

US Standard	US Standard (ounces)	Metric (Approx.)
2 tablespoons	1 fl oz	30 ml
¼ cup	2 fl oz	60 ml
½ cup	4 fl oz	120 ml
1 cup	8 fl oz	240 ml
1 ½ cups	12 fl oz	355 ml
2 cups or 1 pint	16 fl oz	475 ml
4 cups or 1 quart	32 fl oz	1 L
1 gallon	128 fl oz	4 L

Oven Temperatures

Fahrenheit (F)	Celsius (C) (Approx)
250°F	120°C
300°F	150°C
325°F	165°C
350°F	180°C
375°F	190°C
400°F	200°C
425°F	220°C
450°F	230°C

Volume Equivalents (Dry)

US Standard	Metric (Approx.)
¼ teaspoon	1 ml
½ teaspoon	2 ml
1 teaspoon	5 ml
1 tablespoon	15 ml
¼ cup	59 ml
½ cup	118 ml
1 cup	235 ml

Weight Equivalents

US Standard	Metric (Approx.)
½ ounce	15 g
1 ounce	30 g
2 ounces	60 g
4 ounces	115 g
8 ounces	225 g
12 ounces	340 g
16 ounces or 1 pound	455 g

References and Resources

Dashti, Hussein M et al. "Long-Term Effects of a Ketogenic Diet in Obese Patients." *Experimental & Clinical Cardiology* 9.3 (2004): 200–205. Print.

Emmerich, Maria. "Home – Landing Page." *Keto-Adapted*, keto-adapted.com/.

Galgano, F., Favati, F., Caruso, M., Pietrafesa, A. and Natella, S. (2007), The Influence of Processing and Preservation on the Retention of Health-Promoting Compounds in Broccoli. Journal of Food Science, 72: S130–S135. doi:10.1111/j.1750-3841.2006.00258.x

Newman, John C. *Ketogenic Diet Reduces Midlife Mortality and Improves Memory in Aging Mice.* Cell Metabolism, www.cell.com/cell-metabolism/fulltext/S1550-4131(17)30489-8+.

Oey, Indrawati, et al. "Does High Pressure Processing Influence Nutritional Aspects of Plant Based Food Systems?" *Trends in Food Science & Technology*, Elsevier, 23 Sept. 2007, www.sciencedirect.com/science/article/pii/S0924224407002749.

Kosinski, Christophe, and François R Jornayvaz. "Effects of Ketogenic Diets on Cardiovascular Risk Factors: Evidence from Animal and Human Studies." *Nutrients*, vol. 9, no. 517, 2017.

Volek, Jeff S., et al. *The Art and Science of Low Carbohydrate Living: an Expert Guide to Making the Life-Saving Benefits of Carbohydrate Restriction Sustainable and Enjoyable.* Beyond Obesity, 2011.

Volek, Jeff S., and Stephen D. Phinney. *The Art and Science of Low Carbohydrate Performance.* Beyond Obesity LLC, 2012.

Zajac, Adam et al. "The Effects of a Ketogenic Diet on Exercise Metabolism and Physical Performance in Off-Road Cyclists." *Nutrients* 6.7 (2014): 2493–2508. *PMC.* Web. 18 Nov. 2017.

Ziauddin, K.Syed. "Observations on Some Chemical and Physical Characteristics of Buffalo Meat." *Meat Science*, Elsevier, 14 Oct. 2003, www.sciencedirect.com/science/article/pii/0309174094901481

Zinn, Caryn, et al. "Ketogenic Diet Benefits Body Composition and Well-Being but Not Performance in a Pilot Case Study of New Zealand Endurance Athletes." *Journal of the International Society of Sports Nutrition*, BioMed Central, 12 July 2017, jissn.biomedcentral.com/articles/10.1186/s12970-017-0180-0.

Recipe Index

Complete Index

Want MORE healthy recipes for FREE?

Double down on healthy living with a full week of fresh, healthy salad recipes. A new salad for every day of the week!

Grab this bonus recipe ebook **free** as our gift to you:

http://salad7.hotbooks.org

CPSIA information can be obtained
at www.ICGtesting.com
Printed in the USA
BVOW10s0753100118
504937BV00003B/22/P